The Border

Personal Reflections from Ireland North and South

Edited by
Paddy Logue

Oak Tree Press
Dublin

Oak Tree Press
Merrion Building
Lower Merrion Street
Dublin 2, Ireland
www.oaktreepress.com

A catalogue record of this book is
available from the British Library.

ISBN 1 86076 156 9

The views expressed in the articles and the introductory
descriptions of the authors are the opinions of the authors
themselves and do not necessarily express the views of the
Area Development Management/ Combat Poverty Agency/
Northern Ireland Voluntary Trust partnership.

Printed in the Republic of Ireland
by Colour Books Ltd.

Contents

Introduction by Paddy Logue 1

Gerry Adams, Sinn Féin President 11

Esmond Birnie, Ulster Unionist Party Assembly
    Member.. 17

Rev. Pat Buckley, Bishop 20

Gregory Campbell, Democratic Unionist Party
    Assembly Member 24

Seamus Deane, Writer 27

Polly Devlin, Writer 30

Sammy Douglas, Community Worker...................................32

Hugh Frazer, Director, Combat Poverty Agency...................36

Lord Anthony Gifford, Human Rights Lawyer..................... 40

Fred Halliday, Professor of International Relations 43

David Hewitt, Evangelical Christian.....................................46

Mary Holland, Journalist...49

Jennifer Johnston, Writer 52

Margaret Johnston, MBE, Bowler 54

Dennis Kennedy, Lecturer in European Integration.............55

Sister Stanislaus Kennedy, Campaigner for the
Homeless 59

Tony Kennedy, Director, Co-operation Ireland 62

Avila Kilmurray, Director, Northern Ireland Voluntary
Trust..66

Maeve Kyle, Athlete 70

Terence A. Larkin, Businessman 71

Bernadette McAliskey, Civil Rights Campaigner 75

Nell McCafferty, Journalist..79

Eamonn McCann, Journalist 83

Felicity McCartney, Community Worker 86

Ian McCracken, Cross-Border Community Worker..............89

Mamo McDonald, Community Worker...................................93

Geoff MacEnroe, Joint CBI/IBEC Council 100

Ann McGeeney, Joint Manager, Peace and
Reconciliation Programme..104

Aideen McGinley, Chief Executive, Fermanagh Council.....108

Paddy McGinn, Joint Manager, Peace and
Reconciliation Programme.. 110

Justice Catherine McGuinness, Judge of the Irish High
Court 115

Frank McGuinness, Playwright 119

Susan McKay, Journalist 120

Tommy McKearney, Former Republican Prisoner 123

Martin Mansergh, Special Adviser to the Taoiseach on
Northern Ireland..126

Contents

vii

Gary Mitchell, Playwright 129

Paddy Monaghan, Catholic Evangelist 131

Ellen Mongan, Pre-school Teacher and Traveller 135

Christy Moore, Singer 137

Austen Morgan, Lawyer 138

Jane Morrice, Women's Coalition Assembly Member 142

Paul Muldoon, Poet 144

Dervla Murphy, Writer 149

Nuala O'Faolain, Journalist 154

Ardal O'Hanlon, Comic Actor 158

Sir George Quigley, Businessman 161

Janet Quilley, Quaker 165

Ruairi Quinn, Labour Party Leader 168

Derek Reaney, Cross-Border Community Worker 172

Mary Reid, Community Worker 175

Rev. Dr Andrew Rodgers, Senior Presbyterian
    Minister 178

Nick Ross, TV Presenter 182

Rev. Kenneth Wilson, President of Methodist
    Church in Ireland 186

This book is dedicated to the endurance and resilience of the communities of the Border region and to the vision and commitment of the peoples of the European Union who gave to these communities the resources and confidence to reach out to each other after years of conflict and neglect through the Special Support Programme for Peace and Reconciliation.

Introduction

Paddy Logue

I'm not saying that Thales of Miletus, who lived at the beginning of the sixth century BC, was the first cross-border worker of all time, although he did earn his living by measuring and dividing land. What I'm saying is that he was the first European philosopher and his claim to the title rests on the question that he asked: "What is matter?" It is a question which still exercises the minds of our most brilliant contemporary quantum physicists and cosmologists and remains for the most part unanswered.

The "what" question is primitive. It's baby's first question. And like many simple questions, it is difficult to answer. "When" the Border came into existence and "how" it came to be are easy enough. Even the twentieth century's favourite question, the "why" question, which has given rise to the century's characteristic successes in the arts and the study of human behaviour, is easy when it comes to the Border. Admittedly, the "where" question can be a bit tricky, especially "where the Border ran down the middle of the street" (Paul Muldoon). But the "what" question? That's the hard one. And that's the one I put to our contributors: "What is the Border?"

One hundred potential contributors were selected. This was not done on a scientific basis and another editor would have picked equally interesting people. They included nine who were essentially outsiders, although by virtue of their family background or track record of work, they had strong Irish credentials. Of the rest, 51 were perceived Catholics, 40 perceived Protestants; 55 from the North and 36 from the South; and 61 men and 39 women. The editorial aim was to achieve balance, to target the broadest and most inclusive spread of views, to include the well-known with the less well-known, to mix the mainstream with the radical and to avoid repetitious or knee-jerk statements. I encouraged each contributor to keep within 800 words and most did. Where they chose to ignore me, I simply gave in. It is an indication of the quality, sincerity and relevance of the contributions that none was rejected or edited.

The overriding goal was to create a challenging debate about one of our most enduring and sensitive institutions. Some refused the invitation almost immediately. Others agonised and refused later. Some chose to ignore the correspondence. Most refusals were on the basis of sheer pressure of time. A few needed a little cajoling. Those who did contribute put a lot of serious thought and time into it and, I believe, courage. It is not an easy thing to put on public record your thoughts about an issue which has dominated Irish history in this century and, in recent years, occasioned the deaths of 3,000 of your fellow citizens.

The idea of producing the book was not academic or voyeuristic. It was inspired by the practical needs of Border people, cross-border workers and cross-border policy-makers to take a cold, fresh look at the Border and what it means to people at the end of the twentieth century. Indeed, the book arose directly from the experience gained in the implementation of the European Union Special Support Programme for Peace and Reconciliation. The Programme was set up by the European Commission in conjunction with the British and Irish Governments as part of their response to the opportunities and needs that emerged from the changed situation following the cease-fires of 1994.

The Programme aims to reinforce progress towards a peaceful and stable society and to advance reconciliation by promoting urban and rural regeneration, by developing cross-border co-operation, by extending social inclusion, by stimulating economic regeneration and by increasing employment.

One of the Programme's measures is devoted specifically to reconciliation by facilitating cross-border community contact and co-operation of every kind, but especially between communities which are socially excluded. Since 1996, over 600 cross-border community projects have been supported, representing an allocation of £15 million in funds. The projects are assessed and the funds allocated by a unique cross-border partnership between Area Development Management/Combat Poverty Agency (ADM/ CPA) in the Republic of Ireland and the Northern Ireland Voluntary Trust (NIVT) in Northern Ireland. Also represented on this partnership are Co-operation Ireland, Rural Community Network, Community Relations Council, International Fund for Ireland and Local Authorities.

The considerable number and variety of cross-border engagements supported by the Programme raised many questions for the participants about the history, purpose, economics, politics and impact of the Border that they hadn't asked themselves before. Frankly, until they had begun to get involved in cross-border work, they had simply taken the Border for granted. They felt that these questions should become part of a public interaction with individuals and agencies with a policy-making role and also with the general public. This book will contribute to that interaction.

While there are many interpretations of the Border among cross-border workers, there is an agreed view of its main social characteristic and this forms the rationale for cross-border co-operation. All sociological research — governmental, academic, private and voluntary — argues that the Border region is the most deprived in Ireland. Coincidentally, this is also the region most strikingly affected by the conflict both physically and psychologically.

Neglect is a characteristic of most border regions. If the nations of Europe are viewed as a series of pyramids, with power and wealth centralised and concentrated at the apex, it is not surprising that the border regions that lie around the bases of these pyramids will be troughs of neglect, deprivation and stagnation. Quite simply, "back-to-back" development (i.e. London developing the region up to a line from one side and Dublin developing the region up to the same line from the other side) has failed the Border region.

A new face-to-face strategy is required to meet the needs of the socially excluded Border people and to advance the process of peace and reconciliation. Some creaking of the joints can be expected as we turn slowly to face each other. After all, both sides of the Border have been studiously ignoring each other, if not in fact opposing each other, for most of the century. It is challenging. But the volume of cross-border work already funded has developed methods and a staged process of cross-border work which makes it intelligible, manageable and non-threatening.

There are three stages in this process. They are not self-contained stages that must be completed before one moves to the next stage. The typical picture is complex, where different participants in a single project are at different stages and the management task is to proceed at a pace which brings all along comfortably.

The first stage of the process is contact. This is a time of getting to know you, of making acquaintance, of building up confidence. Information is exchanged and meetings organised with little on the agenda other than conversation. The main focus at this stage is mutual understanding. There is a tendency to concentrate on matters of common interest. This is important but can be overdone. It is vital to give the matters which divide the same amount of time and attention. It is only when people are clear about differences and trust the honesty of the other participants that they feel safe. And it is only when they feel safe that they can move forward.

The next stage is co-ordination and it is marked by comparison and joint ventures. This involves explaining how both sides do things, how they finance their work and the values that inspire this work. They listen to the other side's story. They pick out the strengths and weaknesses, the common values and objectives and examine how their services and performance can be improved. They visit each other's projects and form working relationships. They plan joint ventures, which can be as humble as a day-trip for the parents' and toddlers' club. Organisationally, they remain separate within their own structure and with their finances under their own control. This stage represents an advance on contact and may, but not necessarily, lead on to co-operation.

Co-operation is no longer a grouping of a series of perspectives but a coming together of all participants into a single focus. Together they look at the needs of the cross-border region in question and they elaborate a single programme to target these needs. They share aims and objectives, share resources and set up a joint cross-border organisation or structure to implement the programme. This common focus applies to community groups, business ventures or statutory bodies alike. The work might be community care, road building, product marketing, nursery education and the like. It is this degree or quality of cross-border work that our European colleagues describe properly as "cross-border co-operation".

While cross-border co-operation is a relatively recent activity in Ireland (mostly supported by Co-operation Ireland, the EU Interreg Programme and the business sector), the Peace and Reconciliation Programme is currently giving it an enormous boost, particularly among the community and voluntary sector at grass roots level. By contrast, continental Europeans have been active in cross-border work since the 1940s. The Dutch/German cross-border EUREGIO project is a good example. The Dutch/German Border has existed since the Peace of Westphalia in 1648, which brought the bitter religious Thirty Years War to an end (remind you of anything?). In the aftermath of another bitter war, the Second World

War, the embedding of the peace took the undramatic shape of sports exchanges, school trips and social events. The Border people had to learn that "you can't make a German out of a Dutchman and vice versa". And you shouldn't even try. Today they have an elected Council, which administers some public services, job creation and training in their cross-border region to the benefit of both peoples.

The European Charter for Cross-Border Co-operation was adopted as far back as 1981 and represented a considerable track record of cross-border work as well as being an impetus for much more. Ireland is at the beginning of a long process. It is just emerging from a bitter conflict. Until the referendums in 1998 which accepted the principle of consent, the Irish Border has been disputed. While economic and social considerations will urge the people of this island to proceed with enthusiasm, political realities will urge caution. They can learn much from their European colleagues' history and experience of cross-border work, from their humble beginnings in the 1940s to their contemporary ideals of union and integration.

The Irish Border is not as old as the Dutch/German border. But it's older than many of us realise. To have significant memories of living in an Ireland without a Border, one would have to be 100 years old. Soon there will be no one left in Ireland who was born before the Border came into existence.

Once the Boundary Commission wound up in 1925, the Border was here to stay. For some in the North, it is a barrier that protects them from poverty and popery. For some in the South, it is a barrier that protects them from violence and sectarianism. For others on the island, it's a barrier to unity, peace and prosperity. For some, it is an international frontier. For others, it is a minor, local irritant. Many have died attacking it, others have died defending it. It is clear that the Border, like other barriers of skin, gender, religion and place, has thrown up its quota of ignorance, prejudice and phobia. All people on this island live in its shadow. Until very recently, most Irish people tended to identify themselves politically and culturally, and were identified as such by others, by their attitude to the Border.

It is to bridge this barrier, to build sustainable relationships across it, that cross-border reconciliation aims.

For nationalists, there is no ideological problem with the idea or practice of cross-border work and some have taken to it with enthusiasm and some success. But there are difficulties relating to mutual understanding, different ways of doing things, different jurisdictions, different administrative structures, different currencies, to name but some. There are also tensions between the nationalist people of Northern Ireland and the nationalist people of the Republic of Ireland which sometimes take crude forms. Southerners abandoned their Northern kith and kin and stood idly by. Northerners are violent and sectarian and, despite the rhetoric, are content with a "British" way of life which includes superior health care, education provision and benefits. Some community groups from the nationalist community have simply turned away from the challenges and demands of working cross-border.

For unionists, serious ideological resistance compounds the inherent difficulties. Some unionists have stated that cross-border reconciliation is a "united Ireland by the back door". Other unionists are less distrustful and have agreed to approach cross-border reconciliation with an open mind. They have, for example, agreed to the setting up of the cross-border bodies. This is a sensitive area and a few ground-rules have already emerged for unionists willing to get involved in cross-border work:

- The association of the Border region and poverty should be considered more a de facto than a causal relationship.

- The Border should be seen as firm but permeable: the firmer the Border is, the more permeable or "crossable" it is.

- Cross-border projects that include an East-West orientation with Britain as well as a North-South relationship are more acceptable.

- If there is a precedent from another European border region, it is acceptable here also.

In short, unionists say, the Border is not a bad thing. It does not cause poverty. It is as firm as any other international frontier. Cross-border co-operation is not just about North/South relations; it's about British/Irish relations as well. Good practice from other European border regions can be replicated here. The paradox for unionists is that the firmer the Border is, the more permeable it is. And the more permeable it is, the less important it appears to be.

I detect in all this cross-border work the faintest trace of a new constituency similar to the North, the West, the South. It is the Border. It is the constituency of people who live in the towns and countryside that lie adjacent to the Border. It is the people who live on the margins of the two states in Ireland, who more than any other have suffered

structural neglect from both governments. It is the people
who more than any other have borne the brunt of the conflict and endured the greatest disruption. And it is down to
us, the Border people, the rural and the urban, the nationalist and the unionist, the Northerner and the Southerner,
to make common cause in raising the issues of our social
exclusion and reconciliation with the two governments
and the European Union. It is down to us to exploit jointly
and energetically the talents and resources and opportunities of our Border region. Cross-border co-operation is
an idea whose time has come.

I thank the contributors. They are busy people; their
articles were requested during the holiday months; they
made the time to think afresh about the Border and had
the courage to share their thoughts with the public. The
articles range from the anecdotal to the analytic to the
tongue-in-cheek. Every single article contains a truth
about the Border and yet all the articles put together do
not contain the whole truth about the Border. They re-
semble a collage of snapshots of the Border taken from
different angles and in different qualities of light. I'm not
going to preview them here. They speak for themselves.
The readers will decide whether they are living in a time of
change or not.

I also thank the joint ADM/CPA and NIVT editorial
team for their suggestions, enthusiasm and good sense.

Finally, I thank the ADM/CPA administrative staff in
the offices of the Peace and Reconciliation Programme at
Monaghan and Letterkenny, who handled with skill and
good humour all the research, correspondence, typing,
filing and telephone queries.

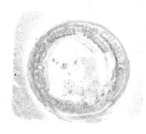

Gerry Adams

Gerry Adams is President of Sinn Féin and MP for West Belfast. Since the mid-1980s, he has led Sinn Féin on a peace strategy which culminated in the Good Friday Agreement of 1998.

When I was a young boy our family would be shushed into silence as our parents watched faltering TV news footage of a bridge wrecked by bombs. These occasional grainy images would be projected into our living room on our black-and-white Radio Rentals television set. While my father listened to news of the latest "outrage", stern-faced peelers looked out at us from outside sandbagged Border barracks. We children had no real sense of what all this was really about. Belfast was far from the Border, though at one point when a posse of peelers surrounded our house and stomped loudly through the uncarpeted wooden-floored bedrooms, it was as if the Border had come home. We knew instinctively that the raid and partition were interconnected.

Later, when college gangs of us went on summer scholarship excursions to the Donegal Gaeltacht, we were disappointed to find no obvious signs of the Border. We were only comforted by the discovery of a mysterious no-man's-land — a vague and questionably guessable distance of road between two states whose existence wasn't even certain but dependent only on whether we believed Seamie

Green, who first informed us about this phenomenon. Crossing the actual Border was in itself an uncertain and loudly debatable event.

"We're over now."

"Nawh we're not. It's coming now. At that big tree! Now."

Our bus swayed gently and Brother Beausang smiled at our dubious geographical assertions as we peered out noisily at an unchanged and unchanging landscape.

"We're in the Free State," someone hollered.

"We're still in the North," exclaimed someone else.

"Sure Donegal is in the north."

"I mean in the six counties."

"Don't be stupid. This is the Free State. Look. That post box is green."

And so it was.

Like all modern states, Ireland has its fair share of divisions — geographical, physical, religious, emotional, cultural, gender, economic and of course political.

Some of these we are only vaguely aware of, but "The Border" is one which imposes its presence on all aspects of our daily lives, whether we live on Rathlin Island or in Cork, in Belfast or in Galway.

It is a deep scar which meanders its way for hundreds of kilometres across our island. It is one of the most criminal of a long line of crimes committed by successive English governments in Ireland. Ireland is historically, culturally and geographically one single unit. The partition of Ireland, established by the British "Government of Ireland Act" and subsequent British Acts, divides Ireland into two artificial statelets, the boundaries of which were determined by a sectarian headcount. It is only now, through the constitutional and institutional elements of the Good Friday Agreement, that these British Acts are being dismantled.

As the English writer C.P. Scott wrote, Ireland was partitioned "to entrench the six counties against nationalist Ireland. Its effect will not be to make a solution of the Irish question easier but harder by creating a fresh and powerful obstacle."

Within the six counties, a divisive, violent and sectarian system of apartheid has held sway since partition. Catholics are still two and a half times more likely to be unemployed and a recent report by the North's Statistics and Research Agency has shown that a Catholic family's average monthly income is £200 less than that of a Protestant family. Moreover, 28 per cent of Catholics' average weekly income is made up of social security benefit, compared to 18 per cent for Protestants. This is not to say that the Protestant working classes are well off. On the contrary, sections share a common economic, as well as a class, condition with their Catholic neighbours.

Inequality, injustice and discrimination permeate all aspects of the Northern state, impacting in every conceivable way on the quality of life of people.

In the 26 counties, the instinct is to look at the Border region, witness the economic disparity with the rest of the South and assume that "The Border" only affects those counties that link it.

But partition, and the political instability and conflict which it creates, has inhibited economic growth beyond simply the Border counties; it has undermined the wider justice system and has wasted valuable resources defending a partitionist structure which all democrats and good governments should be actively seeking to dismantle.

Specifically, the Southern Border counties have endured decades of systematic underdevelopment by an over-centralised narrow-focused Dublin government. A recent study by the Combat Poverty Agency on Rural Poverty in Ireland showed that it was the Border regions that were the most deprived in the Southern state.

In the North, a unionist regime at Stormont, and a unionist-dominated bureaucracy within the Northern Ireland Office, have deliberately favoured development in the eastern counties. Partition has divided the natural economic region of the whole island. The six counties are on the periphery of not only the island economy, as well as the British economy, but also the European economy, making economic development even more precarious. The net result has been needless emigration, depopulation, unemployment and ongoing economic underdevelopment.

It is also quite clear that economic activity and co-operation is hampered not least because of the two tax regimes that operate. This creates inefficiencies and ultimately costs jobs.

Ideologically, Sinn Féin is an Irish Republican Party. We want an end to British jurisdiction in our country and a 32-county-based Irish Republic to replace the two states that have existed since the island was partitioned. We want an end to partition.

That primary objective guides our peace strategy; it has determined our approach during the negotiations leading to the Good Friday Agreement, and now guides our approach to the ongoing negotiations around the efforts to implement the Good Friday Agreement.

There have been obvious attempts to breach the social, economic and cultural barriers created by "The Border" — most obvious through the various European Union initiatives, as well as through the International Fund for Ireland and similar programmes. Specifically, Sinn Féin has argued that Ireland should be organised, and dealt with in the European Union, as a single island economy. We have proposed a series of economic corridors between Donegal and Derry, between Derry and Fermanagh and a corridor linking Sligo with Fermanagh/Tyrone, as well as the Belfast–Dublin corridor, as one way of redressing the imbalance.

For Sinn Féin, the Good Friday Agreement is a transitional arrangement. The interlocked and interdependent elements of the Agreement, which relate to the island as a whole, will break down the Border by bridging the political, economic, cultural and social divides.

That remains Sinn Féin's focus: ending partition — dismantling a Border that has divided our people and subverted our potential to create wealth and prosperity and a lasting peace. I believe we will achieve that goal.

Partition was, and remains, the main means by which equality is denied and the principal method by which self-determination is withheld from us. Partition aborted a national independence struggle in the 1920s, secured Britain a toehold in a part of Ireland from which London could influence all of Ireland; it divided the people of our island into two states, and within one state it established a unionist monopoly which divided us once more.

All that is changing. Much of it has already changed. As we go into a new century, this much at least is certain. Partition has failed.

And the failure is not restricted to the six counties. There are few who will argue that the 26 counties fulfil the needs of the people of this island. Fortunately, the Southern state has escaped the worst of the 30 years of conflict which has raged mostly in the North, though two bomb attacks in Monaghan and Dublin, which claimed 33 lives, was the largest number of people killed in one day.

It is little wonder that James Connolly warned that if partition was imposed it would "mean a carnival of reaction both North and South, would set back the wheels of progress . . ."

Neither has the Celtic Tiger solved all problems. One-third of citizens survive below poverty level. The series of revelations emanating from various tribunals and enquiries illustrate the other end of the scale, with collusion between banks, big business, financial institutions and some senior politicians drawn from all the conservative parties who have actively conspired to defraud taxpayers and prevent the equitable distribution of wealth.

So there are lots of reasons to rid ourselves of partition. I believe we have made a real start to that job of work. The harder we work at it, the more we win people around to the position, the sooner we will achieve that goal.

Esmond Birnie

Esmond Birnie is an Ulster Unionist Assembly Member for South Belfast and Party Spokesman on North-South relations and the British-Irish Council. A writer and economist, in 1999 he published The Northern Ireland Economy *(Ashgate), and "The Economics of Unionism and Nationalism" in P. Roche and B. Barton (ed.),* The Northern Ireland Question *(Ashgate, pp. 139–162).*

In some ways, the Border is not the important thing. That may seem a shocking statement for those who assume that unionism is an inherently negative creed dedicated simply and solely to "keeping the Border".

The Irish Border is, however, the by-product of the exercise of consent by two peoples: those of Northern Ireland and those of the Republic of Ireland. That is its cause. Not some hideous plot by British imperialists to divide the island. It is of course true that, in 1921 and since, sizeable minorities found themselves, *both* North and South, on the "wrong" side of that Border. This was regrettable but probably inevitable.

Almost all of the new central and eastern European countries which came into being post-1918 also contained minority problems. Such ethnic tensions in Poland, Czechoslovakia and Yugoslavia precipitated conflict at the start of the Second World War and now, tragically, they have done so again 50 years later. The correct response is not to try to remove such borders but to maintain equality of treatment for all citizens. The EU and the Council of Europe confirm this and NATO's 1999 war with Serbia was fought over this issue. The institutions of the Belfast

Agreement attempt to recognise both this principle along with that of self-determination and consent.

Just as I as an Ulster Unionist am a partitionist, so I believe the bulk of public opinion in the South is also partitionist. Most people in the Republic of Ireland have decided that the maintenance of the Border is also in their best interests.

Contrary to a number of claims made in the 1990s, the Border is not a huge barrier to economic progress. No convincing evidence has been produced to prove that it is a substantial friction to trade. The extent of economic integration between Northern Ireland and the Republic is in some regards greater than that with Great Britain. In the early 1990s, Northern Ireland manufacturing firms sold three times more goods per capita to the Southern Irish market as they did to Great Britain.

It is perhaps significant that dislocation caused by the Border is not mentioned at all in Cormac Ó Gráda's (1994) authoritative *Economic History of Ireland, 1780–1939*. Exports and imports across the Border are currently 3–5 per cent of the Northern Ireland or Republic of Ireland GDP. Some of the trade flows among the Scandinavian or between the Spanish and Portuguese economies are not dissimilar — for example, in 1986 Spanish exports to Portugal were 2.2 per cent of its total GDP and in 1997 still only 5.4 per cent; and Portugal's population is about three times that of the Republic and six times that of Northern Ireland.

The Border did divide that which hitherto had been united (during the period of British Union, 1801–1921). Some felt sad about this. Certainly, there was an Irish unionist case, personified to some degree by Carson, which opposed Home Rule in 1912–14, not to exclude Ulster but to keep all of Ireland together within the Empire. At the end of the day, it was the Ulster unionist approach which prevailed. History cannot be readily reversed. The old, pre-1921, United Kingdom is not likely to be recreated. Nevertheless, the high degree of interpretation between the 26 counties and the UK has continued since 1921. In some regards, they are not really foreign countries to each other. I may feel more at home on O'Connell Street than on Berlin's Unter den Linden, though this is because I am an ideological heir to Carson rather than Pearse. The British-Irish Council is an attempt to recognise the special East-West relationship.

The Border should in no way preclude friendly co-operation between two equally legitimate states. Once again, the institutions of the Belfast Agreement are an attempt to foster such good neighbourliness and provide mechanisms for soundly based working together on social and economic projects. They may even allow some to accommodate their sense of Irishness with Northern Ireland's continuing place within the United Kingdom.

To sum up, the Border should be firm (i.e. fixed and universally recognised) in conformity with international law and European practice, but also permeable (not a barrier to movements of people, culture and goods). If a historic compromise is to be forged between nationalism, republicanism and unionism, it will have to include this element.

Bishop Pat Buckley

Pat Buckley is a dissident Catholic Bishop. He was re-
moved from his parish by Cardinal Cathal Daly for being
overly involved in community work and for criticising
the Catholic Church in the media. Since 1986, he has had
an independent ministry based at Larne and is the unof-
ficial chaplain to Ireland's increasing number of alien-
ated Catholics. He has recently announced that he is gay.

I was born south of the Border and lived there for 26 years
in Dublin and in counties Carlow, Offaly and Waterford. I
have worked north of the Border for the past 21 years in
inner-city Belfast — at Divis Flats on the Falls Road — in
rural County Down and in urban County Antrim. I cross
the Border at least once a week and my ministry takes me
to every nook and cranny on the island. I find the so-
called Border both artificial and offensive.

I have always been highly critical of the confessional
Catholic nature of the Irish Republic and its 1937 Constitution. Constitutionally, Protestants were discriminated
against and this, aligned with the Catholic Church's big-
oted rules on mixed religion marriages, has contributed to
the decline of the Protestant population in the Republic
form 12 to 3 per cent of the overall population. Having
said that, however, I think that it is worth noting that the 3
per cent Protestant population of the Republic own 27 per
cent of its wealth!

The Republic has changed beyond recognition in recent years. I never thought that I would see that change in
my lifetime. It has become more and more a modern
secular and pluralist state and the power of the Catholic

Church has been greatly and magnificently reduced. At last, the people and the politicians are able to stand up to the bishops and the clergy. The disempowering of the Catholic Church has been greatly helped by all the Church scandals — Bishop Eamon Casey, Father Michael Cleary, Father Brendan Smyth and Father Sean Fortune, etc. Oh happy fault!

Northern Ireland, from partition in 1922, was the opposite. It was deliberately a Protestant statelet for a Protestant people. The governments were anti-Catholic and anti-nationalist. The police were savagely anti-Catholic and anti-nationalist. Catholics and nationalists were second-class citizens and were discriminated against, especially in housing and employment. Even today in Northern Ireland there are two and a half Catholics unemployed for every unemployed Protestant.

But again, great progress has been made in recent years. The prejudiced Stormont parliament is no more. The RUC is undergoing a total transformation into the Northern Ireland Police Service. Catholic housing is at least as good as Protestant housing. And all the fair employment legislation is beginning to achieve parity in employment.

The old Catholic Republic is on its death bed, taking its last ugly gasps. And 100 miles up the road, the old Protestant Ulster is on its death bed — wriggling resentfully and angrily as its days are coming quickly to a close.

These are the best two funerals Ireland will ever celebrate!

The artificial Border created in 1922 was allowed to come into being by two narrow-minded nationalisms — the narrow Catholic nationalism of the southern 26 counties, its people and religious and political leaders and the narrow Protestant nationalism of the six northern counties, its people and religious and political leaders. At the time, Ireland was suffering from a cancer — a cancer caused by 800 years of colonialism, plunder, torture, insurrection, rebellion and resistance.

It was always artificial. Ireland, for thousands of years, had never been divided like that before. It even cut the ancient province of Ulster in two — leaving Cavan, Monaghan and Donegal in the Republic.

I really resent it when I hear people talking about Northern Ireland as "Ulster". It's not; it's only two-thirds of Ulster.

People like Ian Paisley want to build a wall right along the Border from Dundalk to Derry. And if that is too expensive, they would like the Border closed and marked with barbed wire! How utterly pathetic, as the rest of us journey towards greater "internationalism" in the European Community, the United Nations, etc.

The Border is an artificial division of an ancient land. In 1922, it was a poorly thought-out and obscene division and on the eve of the third millennium, it is an absolute and nonsensical contradiction.

What's the answer? The answer has to be both faithful to history and tradition and imaginative enough for the future. This is my suggestion:

1. That the British and Irish Governments put Northern Ireland temporarily in the hands of a United Nations peacekeeping force.

2. That everybody on the island and in Britain reconstruct a four-province Ireland — Leinster, Munster,

    Connaught and Ulster (containing Donegal, Monaghan and Cavan).

3. That each province have its own provincial parliament (to replace the stupid and expensive plethora of councils) in Dublin, Cork, Galway and Belfast.

4. That a new secular and pluralist constitution be drawn up for the whole island.

5. That there be a national assembly at an agreed place (not Dublin or Belfast).

6. That there be a Council of the Islands to regulate Anglo-Irish relations.

Some people say that this is only a dream. My answer is this: "Is my dream not better than the current nightmare"?

The Border, like the Berlin Wall, symbolises all that is bad about all our pasts. Its removal, like the removal of the Berlin Wall, will open the way to the future. We don't need the traditional "United Ireland". We need a "New Ireland".

Gregory Campbell

Alderman Gregory Campbell was first elected to local government in 1981, and has been re-elected every four years since. He has contested assembly and parliamentary elections on behalf of the Democratic Unionist Party. He was the first elected member to the new Northern Ireland Assembly in 1998. He represents East Londonderry. He is the security spokesman for the DUP and is also one of the senior party officers. Gregory has also written a number of booklets on the question of discrimination against the Protestant community in Northern Ireland: Discrimination: the Truth *(1987),* Discrimination: Where Now? *(1993),* Working Towards 2000 *(1998), as well as* Ulster's Verdict *on the Joint Declaration in 1990–91 and 1996–7.*

The Border: what is it, how do I perceive it and what is its purpose? I suppose those are the relevant questions I had to ask myself when asked to compile an article with a title as general as "The Border".

I well remember several nationalist politicians pointing out to me that the people and land on either side of our Border were remarkably similar and that I did not recognise this; and therefore, their logic concluded, is not Ireland one nation? My answer then, as under this title, was: "Do the land and people on either side of the US/ Canadian border not look very alike? Can I not go to dozens of land frontiers and find similar situations?" There is one very consistent theme throughout virtually all of the scenarios in these other countries: there is an acceptance by the people on each side of the Border that, while they are close to and may live on similar landscapes and even speak the same language, they live in two separate countries. Despite almost 80 years of the factual position on the island of Ireland, nationalists have set their face against accepting that. The Border therefore is a boundary indicating where one nation has its limits; its powers extend thus far, its protection is offered to all of those within that defined area and all of those who live within that border should feel proud to belong to that country. Now some might (and do) say that this wasn't always the case in Ireland; that before partition there was one body of people on the whole island. This, of course, flies in the face of reality on two counts. First, the entire island was part of the United Kingdom and therefore any expression of Irishness within it was but a very wide definition of the inclusive nature of the state. Also, of course, even within that single island as part of the UK, there had still been for hundreds of years a distinct and different northern ethos, culture and outlook which was quite different from the southern part of the island.

I believe that the Border should be a non-threatening limitation. It should not have to be reinforced with huge fortification, nor should it be looked upon as an ugly scar across a map. It ought rather to be the logical delineation between two neighbouring states, it should be a crossing point determining where two separate peoples work at improving relationships to their mutual benefit. In many instances, our border has not been allowed to take on these attributes, not principally because of attitudes adopted by those in favour of it, but because of attitudes and actions of many of those opposed to it.

I view it as an essential demarcation line. It is something which determines my Britishness without diluting anyone else's Irishness. It should be evidence of the continuing commitment to those values that the various regions of the United Kingdom hold. Whether Scots, Cornish, Welsh or Ulster, we each have different and quite unique features within that Kingdom. Those who have campaigned for the Border's removal, whether violently or constitutionally, do so through a fundamental misunderstanding of why unionists support its retention. It is not required to maintain some form of "supremacy". There is no supremacy to maintain, it is not to retain "all power in our own hands", as there hasn't been any power since 1973. It isn't even because the Irish Republic has an ethos that is alien to Protestants. It is there because we are British citizens entitled to whatever benefits British citizenship brings. No amount of changes to the Republic's constitution or modernising of that state can alter this fundamental fact of life for Ulster's unionist people.

Its purpose may well change over the next few years of the new millennium, as the UK and indeed Europe changes. We will need to be able to develop new ways of dealing with that changing reality. Whether we are drawn into some new form of European co-operative arrangement, or a more federal type of super-state begins to emerge, against the wishes of many of us, there is one thing which needs to remain constant: the passionate commitment, the cultural outlook and the ethos of the people of Northern Ireland must not be diminished or diluted as a result of that political evolution.

Seamus Deane

Seamus Deane is Keough Professor of Irish Studies at the University of Notre Dame, a Director of Field Day and a member of the Royal Irish Academy. Among his publications are Selected Poems *(1988);* Celtic Revivals *(1985); A* Short History of Irish Literature *(1986);* The French Revolution and Enlightenment in England 1779–1832 *(1988);* Strange Country *(1997); and a novel,* Reading in the Dark *(1996). He is General Editor of the three-volume* Field Day Anthology of Irish Writing *(1991).*

Border areas are often seen as distinctively different from other inhabited areas. In them, the conventional wisdom has it, we can see more clearly than elsewhere how different cultures or systems interact with one another; or we can see the graded transition from one to another; or we can see that in this border zone, we have a culture that is peculiarly its own, belonging entirely to neither one of the polities that lie beyond it. Possibly, much of this could be said of the Border areas that surround the partition line that divides Ireland into two states. But my own experience of living in what is in effect the Border town of Derry has not bequeathed to me any sense of the diversity or richness that some people profess to find in liminal territories. Rather the reverse.

The most standard nationalist/republican response to the Border in Derry is that it has cut the city off from its natural hinterland of Donegal and has thereby damaged both places. But it is even more important to recognise that the Border reproduces itself in every area within the North. It is and always has been a sectarian border; it em-

braces a fertile progeny of internal borders, all of which
enhance the unnatural, defensive atmosphere of the State.
These are not flexible or porous borders; they are not in-
dicators of a community's autonomy. They are prison
walls. Their function is to immure communities and, with
that, to fossilise the political situation in its original form.
Since the Troubles began, the existence of these borders
has been signalled in every conceivable way by flags, murals, graffiti, painted kerbstones. Indeed, the most publi-
cised effort to break these borders has been that of the Orange Order in its insistence on carrying its demented
marches across every nationalist territory within range, on
the ground that it has a right to walk the Queen's highway.
This is not a breaking but a reaffirmation of borders, and
it is a perversion of any notion of civil rights. The purpose
is to confirm that the internal borders are as fixed as the
external Border; within both, the Orange and unionist as-
cendancy wants to persuade itself that it still rules.

Yet wherever there are contested borders, there is always a symmetry between the attempt to insist on their
fixity and the attempt to insist on their transience. It is
obvious that a whole range of economic activities, from
smuggling to shopping, have their own peculiar dynamic
in border areas. So too with military and security actions.
The Border in Ireland is not one element among others in
the lives of the people who live in its environs. It is the
governing element, capable of creating prosperity or poverty, of increasing the threat of violence, intensifying the
frustrations that accompany blocked roads, bridges and
crossings. But most of all, any border, and the Irish Border in particular, is always a reminder of how arbitrary the
definition of a political community can be when it tries to

express itself in territorial terms. It is also a reminder how crucial that territorial expression can be and how purposeful was the determination behind it.

Derry is a Border town with internal borders that make themselves manifest even in the slash mark between the names Derry/Londonderry; in the sectarian housing estates; in the old walled architecture of the town and in the competing histories of its development from Columba to the Siege to the Battle of Bogside. On the west bank, Donegal is always in the rear-view mirror; from the Waterside, it is County Derry/Londonderry. The Border might seem more "natural" if it coincided with natural boundary features, like a river or a mountain range. But such coincidence is rare with any system of borders. What are the natural Borders that separate the counties of Ireland? Or the dioceses of the Catholic Church or of the Church of Ireland? Or of the various administrative units that make up electoral districts or education board districts? Much of the history of any territory can be understood by learning where its borders once were, what were the townlands and baronies and parishes and demesnes and fiefdoms, council areas or military or police or judicial districts. There is nothing "natural" about borders; they are all created to assert power.

The Border is exactly that: a declaration of power and control. The most unfortunate aspect of the Border's history is that, to survive, it has forever had to insist on its presence. It never therefore became naturalised. If it could have been forgotten about, it would have been more secure. But it can now never be ignored. So it will remain assertive, creating division within the territory it was designed to consolidate.

Polly Devlin

Born into a large family in Northern Ireland, Polly Devlin, OBE, is a writer, broadcaster and conservationist. Her account of an Ulster childhood, All of Us There, *was acclaimed for its lyricism and fine writing. She has also published (among other books)* The Far Side of the Lough, *a collection of short stories (re-issued October 1999);* Dora, *a novel; and a collection of essays,* Only Sometimes Looking Sideways.

It was a sort of trim around the country, somewhere. Near Goraghwood. The policemen came on board the train from Portadown — big men with uniforms who at any moment could make away with you. Goraghwood was like a gorge, high cliffs that the train slid between successfully, every time. There was no town there, no platform, no passengers getting on and off, just the big men in uniforms.

In the kitchen, the wireless was permanently tuned to Radio Éireann. There was another world out there across the Border. In that other world which was called the Freese Tate people danced and spoke more softly, and ate cakes by Gateau, and if you felt like singing, do sing an Irish song.

Every year we went on holiday to Bray. That's when the train stopped at Goraghwood, and after that we were in an Italy of Senses; like Goethe travelling post-haste to see the first glimpse of Italy, so the cement buckets going high across the road in a make-shift funicular at Drogheda were like a sign that we were in the promised land. Ireland. Eire. Éireann. The four green fields, only there were three. Another country where they did things differently and where people were on our side.

In those days, "our side" meant a call for fairness, not extremist positions. We were too young to know the whys and wherefores but we weren't too young not to notice a system of discrimination that drifted like spore from Stormont, that great US Fascist building at Stormont where the Unionist party was in power. No Catholic in the Northern Ireland cabinet, no way to the top. The Border did all this. The bloody Border.

Later, it wasn't anything romantic to do with trains, it was an ugly reality of queues at Border posts, and being photographed in eight seconds and identified as your car tipped the ramp.

When you are a child, things that happened before you were born have never not happened. They were eternal. I now know that the Border had only been in place over 20 years in my childhood, but for it not to be there was unthinkable. It was the Great Divide, so potent, so irrevocable, so there, a no-man's-land lying athwart a brown bare mountain, marked by a couple of huts, a painted pole, a barrier on the road, but that putative line trimmed our lives as well as cutting our country. It hemmed us in, removed our Irishness from us and made us Northern Irish. I know no one who speaks of being Eastern Irish or Western Irish. Not that we ever named what we were. No one asked us. It was only when I came to England that I was asked to define where I was from. By then there was no other definitive. I was irrevocably Northern Irish, as Russians under Stalin or under Communism can never shake off the shadow of the Soviet. I accepted an OBE. What was I thinking of? I wasn't thinking. The recognition came from my place of birth but not from my country. Straddle the line. Be divided. Live on the Border.

It drove a jagged line through our own psyche and personalities. But when those men sat down to draw the line that gave us this prefix Northern, they scored into the very fabric of Ireland and its people. A border is an ornamental word for a cut that scorified a country.

Sammy Douglas

Sammy Douglas has been active in community development and economic regeneration since the mid-1970s. He played a leading role in two important publications: Community Development in Protestant Areas *and* Poverty amongst Plenty. *He is currently involved in a wide range of voluntary activity, including chairing The Greater East Belfast Partnership and co-chair of The Belfast European Partnership Board and is a trustee of the Northern Ireland Voluntary Trust. Sammy lives in East Belfast with his wife Gillian and four children.*

In 1991, I attended a conference in Belfast entitled "Community Development in Protestant Areas". One of the keynote speakers was Shankill Road loyalist, Gusty Spence. In his address he remarked that, for loyalists, politics was, historically, about supporting the state and the continuance of the union with Great Britain. Protestants were always encouraged to vote in order to keep the

Border safe, *"lest it would fall and the Jesuits would move in and all Hell would break loose"*.

I would have heard similar sentiments and fears expressed by many people, in particular the older generation, while growing up in Sandy Row, a fiercely loyalist area of inner-city Belfast. The Free State, or "The South" as it was commonly described, was an alien, Roman Catholic-dominated, Irish Gaelic state "ready to pounce" when the timing was right. Since the inception of Northern Ireland, the looming spectre of a Dublin takeover has been at the heart of Protestant insecurity. Events such as the 1970 Dublin arms trial involving Irish government ministers, periodic rhetoric such as "we will not stand idly by" and Republican attacks mounted with apparent ease from across the Border, have tended to reinforce this conditioning.

Since the early 1990s, I have been involved at a community level in a number of cross-border schemes, ranging from transnational training programmes to community enterprise initiatives. These experiences have helped me personally to dispel many of the perceptions and myths that I had harboured over the years.

One of the most surprising things that I have found is the response of people from the Republic to "the Border question". With the phenomenal success of the "Celtic Tiger", many of the people I have met do not want to absorb Northern Ireland into an all-Ireland Republic. They certainly do not want our problems of poverty and unemployment — not to mention the one million disgruntled Protestants and the UDA/UFF, UVF, Red Hand Commandos, etc!

One of the people who have helped my understanding of life in the Republic is Brian McKevitt of the Cooley Peace Initiative in County Louth, a voluntary group involved in organising initiatives aimed at peace-building through raising awareness of cross-border issues. I have participated in some of these events and have been able to discuss sensitive and highly emotional issues pertaining to "the Troubles", in a spirit of honesty and openness.

A few years ago, I was one of the guest speakers at a conference in Carlingford, which addressed community responses to the paramilitary ceasefires. I was surprised to find a number of Jesuit priests attending, particularly when one of the main topics for discussion was the role of the Orange Order. A female member of the audience accused the Order of being sexist and manipulating Protestant women, whose role on the Twelfth was "to make tea and sandwiches for the men returning from the field". In response, my fellow panelist, a member of the Ulster Unionist Party and a leading figure in the Orange Order, became very defensive that such an accusation should be made against him. He was adamant that this could not be further from the truth, as he, more than most, knew the needs of women. To my shock (and the horror of some in the audience) he revealed that for many years prior to his conversion to Christianity, he had been dressing up in women's clothes. I think we gained a few more partitionists that day!

On a more serious note, as we continue to come out of a bitter 30-year conflict, a number of positive developments have taken place. These, I believe, have helped to change negative perceptions and attitudes towards the Border from sections within the unionist community. The emergence of victim support groups has brought home to us all the pain and hurt that has been inflicted on so many innocent people on both sides of the Border. Alongside this, the referendum to remove the Republic's claim to jurisdiction over Northern Ireland (articles 2 and 3), the Irish government's clampdown on Republican dissidents along the Border after the Omagh bombing and the relative peace arising from the IRA ceasefire have created space and confidence for fresh thinking.

I, for one, am daring to think new things in our relationships with the Irish Republic. For me, there is much to be gained from mutual co-operation and respect. As we hurtle towards a new millennium and with all the social and economic problems likely to emanate from an expanded Europe, surely it is time to put behind us forever, our ancient quarrels and antagonism towards one another? Because after all, despite my numerous cross-border contacts and meetings, I return home to the blue skies of Ulster, as a Protestant, secure in my British and unionist identity!

Hugh Frazer

*Hugh Frazer has been Director of the Combat Poverty
Agency, an Irish government agency, in Dublin for the
past 12 years. Prior to that he worked in Belfast as a
youth and community worker and then as the first Director of the Northern Ireland Voluntary Trust. He has
written and lectured extensively on issue of poverty,
community development and community relations. He is
also a painter of the urban landscape. He is a native of
Cullybackey, County Antrim and is married with three
children.*

For me, the Border is and always has been much more
than a physical space or a line of separation on the map. It
is also a state of mind. It is the place where all the ambi-
guities, contradictions and dilemmas of being both British, Irish and Northern Irish come together. It is thus for
me a place of both opportunity and excitement and of fear
and trepidation. It is where the desire for what is known
and familiar and the fascination and excitement of the
unknown and different collide. For me, the Border can be
a focal point for either a new reconciliation and celebra-
tion of the differences and diversity of culture, politics and
religion on this island, or it can be a continuing physical
and mental barrier that deepens divisions and fosters
separateness both between and within the north and
south.

As a child growing up in a middle-class unionist and
British tradition in the heart of North Antrim in the 1950s
and 1960s, the Border was somewhere distant and remote. We crossed it going on holiday to Donegal or Cork

or Connemara. It was not something that should or should not exist, but just a given reality of life. Crossing it gave me a very real sense of going somewhere different, of going back in time to somewhere poorer, more rural and backward and with different accents, culture and religion, but at the same time exciting, warm and friendly. Very occasionally in some places this was countered by a sense of threat, an anti-British feeling, but we didn't stay long in such places. All this gave me a sense of going to somewhere that was exciting and slightly exotic and to somewhere that was less disciplined and ordered, where imagination and myth could more easily be allowed to roam. But then that is often the feeling I get from travelling to somewhere foreign and unknown and the other side of the Border was definitely foreign — far more so than the much longer and slower journey across the Irish Sea that I frequently made by boat and train to school or relatives in Wales and England.

The actual crossing of the Border accentuated the sense of difference with customs post, bureaucratic forms and triangles on the car windscreen. There was also, when very young, the fear of being arrested on the way home if the undeclared binoculars given to my father by a friend while on holiday were discovered. Happily, they never were, but it added to the sense of excitement and trepidation and above all to the sense of having been somewhere different.

In more recent times, of course, the physical awareness of the Border was reinforced by checkpoints and security measures. But by then, I had been to university in Dublin and increasingly I was becoming aware not of the differences but of the many things in common and the shared history of both parts of the island. At the same time, I also became increasingly aware of how remote and distant the North was for many people in the South and how little contact or understanding there was between people. This seemed and still seems to me ridiculous and absurd on a small island, both parts of which belong to a wider European Community.

When I moved to Dublin in 1987, after working in Northern Ireland for 14 years on issues of poverty, community development and reconciliation, one of my real concerns was to try and encourage more contact and understanding between both parts of the island in the areas in which I was working. But I also recognised that, at least to some extent, I was coming to Dublin as an outsider, more so than if I had come a far greater distance from Cork or Kerry or even Donegal. Happily, much has changed in the last 12 years and there is much greater contact, exchange and mutual learning between policy-makers, community and voluntary organisations and the private sector than there used to be. The peace process has also fostered much more understanding of the political differences and diversities, though there is still a long way to go.

The continuing challenge is to break down barriers and to encourage people to learn from and co-operate with each other across the Border. Success will be when no one needs to see the Border as a defensive line or a line of exclusion and separation and when all traditions feel confident enough to welcome economic, social and cultural co-operation across the Border. Institutionally and politically, the Border may or may not prove to be a permanent reality. Either way, with the increasing globalisation of the world and the integration of Europe, the obsession with national borders is, for me, increasingly an anachronism. I believe that borders, as well as being a line on a map, should be malleable and permeable. They should be seen not as points of division and exclusion but as positive meeting points, points of contact and opportunity. I hope that the Border on this island will increasingly become a catalyst to help us to celebrate and accept the rich and diverse traditions on this island. I hope that it will become a point of interaction which can stimulate new thinking, creativity and imagination and help us to redefine our different identities in an increasingly interdependent world. In that way, we can begin to develop a more inclusive, pluralist and fair society in both parts of this island. I believe that this is beginning to happen and that the only thing that can hold it back or stop it is the recurrence of violence and conflict.

Lord Anthony Gifford

Lord Anthony Gifford practises as a barrister (Queen's Counsel) in London and as an attorney-at-law in Kingston, Jamaica. He has been involved in human rights issues in Britain, Northern Ireland, Southern Africa and the Caribbean. At present he is acting for the family of James Wray at the Bloody Sunday Inquiry. He was a Labour member of the House of Lords before the recent abolition of hereditary peers — which he supported.

My visits to the island of Ireland have mainly been to the North. They have concerned human rights and legal issues arising from the Troubles. My first visit was as a young member of the Society of Labour Lawyers in January 1969, just after the Belfast to Derry march. Vigilantes patrolled the streets by night to protect the residents of the Bogside from raids by the B-Specials. It was a vivid introduction to the realities of life in a city which was meant to be part of my country, but seemed very different.

In subsequent visits to Derry, I have always tried to travel into County Donegal, to the villages along Lough Swilly. In the past, you had to pass the Army checkpoint, but no immigration control or customs. Because of the "common travel area", the Republic of Ireland was a separate state but somehow not a foreign state. The dividing line was a border but not a frontier. It was a border unlike any other in the world.

I have been across borders in other partitioned countries, in Cyprus and Berlin. You had to walk through an eerie no-man's-land. Nothing like that in Ireland. Yet the

Irish Border, quiet as it may seem, has provoked a state of conflict which is as bitter as any in the world.

Another theatre of conflict with which I was much involved was South Africa. There too, borders were manufactured in order to facilitate the dominance of one group of inhabitants over others. Those borders, which delineated the so-called "bantustans", are now gone. After a miracle of transformation and reconciliation, all the inhabitants of South Africa now live within the same border in a democratic society.

If, ten years ago, I was asked to name the three most insoluble problems in the world, I would have answered: apartheid in South Africa, the Arab-Israeli conflict in Israel/Palestine and Northern Ireland. The first has gone; the second is inching towards resolution; and the third, as I write, still hovers between triumph and disaster.

The people of South Africa, especially the oppressed Black people, have given the world an extraordinary lesson in transcending race hatred and building a unified nation. One of the keys was that they showed the Whites that Blacks loved their country as much as Whites. When Thabo Mbeki, now President of South Africa, first met with a delegation of Whites in 1988, he said "I am an Afrikaner". On that basis, he and his movement, the African National Congress, persuaded the Whites that political change did not threaten the cultural traditions, the way of life, of the White minority.

I have no doubt that Protestants and Catholics, north of the Border and south of it, have an equal commitment to the development of their environment. They love to be where they are, even if some love to be Irish and others love to be Ulster men and women. They are all much more interested in development within the island of Ireland than they are in development in London or Manchester. Like the Blacks and Whites in South Africa, they have more in common with each other than with any other set of people.

Having lived through the liberation of Mozambique and Zimbabwe and the tearing down of the Berlin Wall, and having observed the first democratic elections in South Africa, I am an optimist for change in Northern Ireland. But the Border is a wound which will not heal quickly. An agreement of parties to work together does not erase the pain of history.

As in South Africa, reconciliation will come more easily if the horrors of the past are not obscured, but in some measure atoned for. The recovery of the bodies of people killed by the IRA is a part of this atonement. The Bloody Sunday Inquiry should be another. Bringing the killers of Patrick Finucane and Rosemary Nelson to justice would be a third. The relatives of those who died in all these chapters of the conflict, and many others, suffer grief which endures to this day.

The Border is now unpatrolled and unremarkable, yet it is as real in many minds as if it had checkpoints and barbed wire. The mental Border is more potent than the physical. But with goodwill, courage, and the capacity to look over the partition which divides to the common interests which unite, I believe that the mental walls can also be torn down. I salute all those residents of the island of Ireland who are working to make this happen.

Fred Halliday

Professor Fred Halliday was born in Dublin in 1946, and educated at the Marist School, Dundalk, and Ampleforth College, Yorkshire. He has since 1985 been Professor of International Relations at the London School of Economics. He is the author of a dozen books, amongst them studies of the Cold War and of the Middle East.

For the first 16 years of my life my family home was in Dundalk, a few miles from the Border with Northern Ireland, and a town in which, then and now, the tensions of modern Ireland were acutely felt. The *Rough Guide* advises its readers to stay clear of Dundalk on the grounds that it has, for centuries, been an uneasy Border town. But it was the partition of the 1920s that were to mark the town I grew up in. My maternal grandmother was the anchor of our life in Dundalk. As a young girl, she had been presented to Parnell, and, on the death of her husband in the early 1920s, had been given the responsibility for administering the main graveyard, on the Race Course Road, in Dundalk — home, as subsequent reportage never fails to remind us, of an important republican plot.

My own parents came from divergent strands within the modern history of these islands. My mother, one of 14 children of a nationalist family, had seen two aunts taken off to the Crumlin Road in 1916; my father came from a family firm of English shoemakers who had moved their factory and 50 of their staff to Ireland, in the late 1920s, to circumvent the import taxes of the Cosgrave and, later, de Valera governments.

My family was most definitely pro-Treaty, hostile to armed republicans and committed to co-existence with the North. My father was a member of the Dundalk fire brigade which in 1942 went North to help out in Belfast after a particularly devastating German raid. The first time I ever saw a gun designed for killing, as opposed to the hunting rifles that lay around the house, was when the son of Kevin O'Higgins, then a Minister in the Fine Gael government, came to lunch. His bodyguard put his pistol, a very cold grey item, on the kitchen table.

Yet we had, as local custom perhaps dictated, a calculated co-existence with what was always, even in the 1940s, a force in the town, the republican movement. My father's secretary was, for many years, a formidable lady. She was, so I was told, the IRA treasurer and kept the money in her wooden leg. As some kind of insurance policy, my parents made it a point only to hire gardeners who had fought against the Treaty: my earliest experiences were, therefore, of conversations on the lawn with these gnarled, charming and wise veterans of the Curragh internment camp, who, as the practice of the time dictated, were also my babysitters.

This experience was to do much to shape my later view of the world. If I had to account for my interest in international affairs, and for conflicts that run along borders in particular, I would certainly start where my own life began, on the Border between the Irish Republic and what we universally termed "the North". But my first childhood experience, revitalised by experiences of encountering real borders, was of a strange gap, between the border of discourse and the invisible one that existed. When I finally came upon a *real* border, as in Germany, replete with barbed wire, watchtowers and guards, this came as a kind of relief.

To this illusory border was added a second quality, equally powerful, of what did constitute the Border; namely social difference. For if the Border was invisible *as a physical object* it most certainly was visible as a social construct. The moment you passed the Border going northwards you were in a different world: the roads were better, the hedges neater, the houses better painted, the cars more modern. Above all, the shops on the other side of the Border were different: *they* had several kinds of breakfast cereal, we had only Corn Flakes; they had Mars bars, we did not.

To this very day, when I hear the words "Crossmaglen", "Newry", "Enniskillen", I see goods that I do not have. Many years later, I was to develop a theory of the Cold War based not, as many other theories were, on nuclear weapons or strategic conflict, but on the conflict between *social systems*. When the Berlin Wall came down, the East German people flooded over demanding a better life — "kiwis and nectarines", as one put it. Perhaps this theory had its roots in the earlier experience of the Irish Border.

Above all, however, that experience suggests a sort of normative conclusion. The Border *was* totally arbitrary; it did cut society in two, not least sundering Dundalk from its industrial heartland in the North. But no border, even one supposedly "natural", is objectively given. The agreement of 1922 was indeed arbitrary, inaccurate, in some ways unjust. The broader moral may, however, be that it is better to work with such agreements, and try to make the world more just, safe, democratic on each side of the Border. As they say, *pacta sunt servanda*. In this light, Dundalk is a good place to start.

David Hewitt

David Hewitt, CBE, LLB, is married to Margaret and has four children and one grandchild. He is an Evangelical Christian and Presbyterian Elder, a Senior Partner in a Belfast solicitors' practice and a member of the Parades Commission. He is a former Chairman of City of Belfast YMCA, of Sullivan Upper School Governors and of ECONI (Evangelical Contribution on Northern Ireland), an independent assessor of military complaints procedures and an international rugby player.

My head, my heart and my spirit respond differently.

My Head
School history lessons and constitutional law studies at Queen's taught me something about that meandering line across Ireland on my school atlas map of the British Isles. Twenty-six counties were green, and six counties pink like the big island — a political compromise, the best efforts of those in power at one of the crisis points in Anglo-Irish history to balance the demands of nationalists and unionists. Thus the practical implications of sovereignty, jurisdiction and taxation were settled for the time being.

I write on my sixtieth birthday. For the first half of my life, the Border mattered little. It happened to be where British rule stopped and Irish rule started. We on the pink bit were blessed by supporting millions from the London Exchequer. Wasn't it obvious from our superior infrastructure?

Civil rights agitation in the 1960s awakened in me a deep interest in Anglo-Irish politics. Opportunities were created for in-depth discussion with Irish nationalists through membership of the Northern Consensus Group. Prejudice was exposed, perceptions undermined, suspicions removed and truths revealed. Together we accepted that the Border should remain, so long as this was the choice of the majority in Northern Ireland, and provided power was shared and the symbols of government reflected both traditions. My head still says this is not the time to tamper with that meandering line and I am comfortable with my British citizenship. The thought of the upheaval in matters constitutional, legal, social, and financial seems a high price to pay — for what? Sixty-year-olds can do without hassle.

My Heart

If my head resists change, my heart might more easily be swayed. I have always lived in Ireland, albeit on the pink bit. A number of my family have proudly represented Ireland in sport. I honeymooned in Kerry and Connemara. Over 30 years of summer holidays in Donegal have made it my second home. I am an elder of the "Presbyterian Church in Ireland".

Yet my sense of Irishness had to be nurtured. I was secure in my British, unionist, Protestant socialising and mindset, with its inherited suspicion of much that was Irish, nationalist and Roman Catholic. My love of the countryside south and west of the Border could be in-dulged without having to engage with its suspect inhabitants. Their subversive counterparts who lived in our pink bit could generally be avoided. But dialogue with nationalists helped me understand why they wanted space to be Irish, and to be accepted as such. As I listened to deeply committed Irish nationalists who abhorred republican violence, I began to understand what they meant when they spoke of alienation in a state whose official symbolism excluded them. And I gained a new freedom to express my own British Irishness — a freedom that I increasingly value and enjoy. And they listened to me, and were sympathetic to my strongest reason for voting to retain the Border — the bitter legacy of armed-force republican fascism. How could I vote for that which has motivated such cruel barbarity and has sullied Irish nationalism? "The heart has its reasons that reason know not of."

My Spirit

The value system of a Christian should ultimately be shaped by the One who said His kingdom was not of this world. A significant and immediate impact of the coming of the Kingdom of God in Christ was the demolition of the bitter barrier of national identity between Jew and Gentile. The future vision of His kingdom was of people from all nations, and of all colours and political preferences, in perfect unity because of what was effected at a point in history on a cross outside Jerusalem. Tribalism in Ireland has tarnished the Kingdom of God. Both green and orange have sought to sanctify their cause, "shedding blood for mother Ireland" or "for God and Ulster". The murals of East and West Belfast vie with each other in their blas-

phemy, identifying the God of peace with those in bala-
clavas clutching machine guns.

Like many, my pilgrimage has been a long and sometimes uncomfortable path from the security of Protestant,
puritan fundamentalism to the discovery of freedom in
fellowship with fellow Christians "from the other side". I
have no need to shed my reformation convictions, for it is
they that underline the centrality of the Lordship of Christ
and our common faith in Him, and the unimportance of
denominational labels. Nor do I need to shed my unionist
aspirations, so long as they are practised, and informed,
by the values of the Kingdom of God. That meandering
line on the map grows less relevant as the bitter green and
orange sectarianism within Northern Ireland grows more
ugly. Followers of the Prince of Peace have an unavoidable
mandate to oppose bigotry. Others can look after the Border when the time is right.

Mary Holland

Mary Holland is a columnist with The Irish Times *and
Dublin correspondent with* The Observer. *She has won
many awards for her work on TV and in the newspapers.
She has been covering Irish affairs from the beginning of
the Troubles.*

The young Church of Ireland minister sat in his office,
looking across the glittering sweep of the river, to the hills
of Donegal in the distance. They came at night, by boat

from the other side, set fire to the house and went back the same way. He was talking about an IRA attack on one of his parishioners, but could as well have been describing American Indians, waiting in the woods to swoop down on the first settlers in Virginia.

This is what the Border meant — and perhaps still means to many Ulster Protestants living in Fermanagh and Tyrone. It is a defence, a bulwark against enemies who come by stealth in the night. To nationalists living in the same areas, the view is of course very different. The Border has been a daily affront trapping them in a state to which they owe no loyalty and which all too often regards them as hostile.

I have driven the road from Dublin to Derry hundreds of times, in good times and bad. What strikes me most of the time is the heart-stopping beauty of the countryside, the fields of yellow rapeseed, the blue hills, the dignity of the small grey towns. There was a time, during the worst of the violence, when the crossing at Aughnacloy, with its slitted turrets and barbed wire, was something of an ordeal. One never knew if the security forces would decide to search the car, even when there were small children in the back seat.

On one occasion, an over-enthusiastic squaddie wanted to pull off the back doors because a safety device designed to protect children meant that it was impossible to wind the windows right down. "She could have anything hidden in those doors," he said, before his commanding officer, who fortunately had seen these locks before, told him to catch himself on.

But then another time, again with young children in tow, I was driving back to Dublin late at night in the driv-

ing rain when one of the front tyres had a blowout. As I sat
there in near despair ("What are we going to do Mummy?
What's happening?"), someone came towards us, flashing
a torch. It was a young soldier. He and one of his mates
changed the tyre and then brought us all into the Army
post for a cup of tea.

It seems so peaceful now. But many of the memories of
what the Border has meant are more threatening. I remember an IRA funeral in the wild countryside of Tyrone
some time in the 1980s. In Derry or Belfast it was unusual
to see many RUC men or soldiers at such events. They
tended to keep a discreet if watchful distance. But here,
the security presence was overwhelming. There were armoured cars massed in the narrow lanes, helicopters
whirring just above the hedges — or so it seemed. Soldiers
waited with guns ahead in every corner, I half expected
the redcoats to come riding out of the heather.

But there were also occasions of inspiring grace. I will
never forget a Protestant farmer's wife, whose son was
killed when a van carrying him and his work-mates was
blown to bits by the IRA. She told me that she had stayed
up night after night praying on her knees that God would
giver her the strength to forgive her son's killers. She felt
no bitterness and hoped merely that they would see the
error of their ways.

Hopefully, such human pain will become a thing of the
past. Recognising what so many victims have suffered
over the past 30 years, helping each side to understand
the other's stories, giving public expression to human cost
— that is the task which faces us now. Otherwise, some
time in the future, history will again explode in our faces.
Perhaps if we can meet the challenge to cross over the

Border that exists in all our minds, the line on the map
will come to seem less and less important and will at last
disappear.

Jennifer Johnston

*Jennifer Johnston was born in Dublin in 1930. She has
lived in Derry since 1974. She has written and published
11 novels, some short stories and monologues. She is hard
at work on the next novel.*

As a child living in Dublin, I used to skulk around the
grown-ups, listening to their conversations and extrapo-
lating from them the words and notions that caught my
fancy. At that time, the Border appeared to me to be just
another word in the dictionary of our mythology. It de-
noted the only possible ending to all those tales of warriors and heroes, magic and spells, the undefeated men of
the North who beat all comers, who could change themselves at will into snakes or raging torrents or hide themselves in the mystery of madness.

What could be done to protect us, the seemingly more
modest and peaceful people on this island, from the excesses of such people? It seemed only logical to me that
someone should at some stage have built an insurmountable wall, or planted, like in *Sleeping Beauty*, an impenetrable hedge of thorns, stretching for miles and miles, to
keep us safe and the others, the wild ones, contained on
their own side.

I was disappointed when I went once with my grandparents to spend a holiday at the Giant's Causeway to find
nothing more than a couple of huts and some men in what
looked like bus conductors' uniforms. Bits of paper were
stamped and we went on as if nothing momentous had
happened. The people didn't look like heroes and warriors
anymore that we did. We ate the same food, wore the
same clothes and, to all intents and purposes, spoke the
same language. I was puzzled, but wise enough not to ask
silly questions.

Then the war came and once more the Border appeared to me to be a bulwark against come sort of terrible
doom: we were again protected by its presence. Our lights
shone brightly against their darkness. In fact, at that time
the Border was for me not just a protection against the
men of the North, but against the whole world. "Thank
God, we're surrounded by water" the song went . . . and
also the Border!

Of course, I grew out of such childish fantasies and discovered a reality that is far more complex and far more
frightening. The huts are gone now as are the men dressed
as bus conductors, and the Border is seen quite plainly to
be, as it has always been, a wilful construction in people's
heads.

An insurmountable wall?
A hedge of thorns?
Certainly no fairy tale.

In the fairy tale, the prince comes, or the hero, Charming
or indeed Cuchulain, call him what you will, and the

hedge withers and men and women are freed from the spell that was upon them.

As I gaze at the serried ranks of politicians, our Red Branch Knights, daily on the television screen, I find it hard to pick out a hero from among the weary throng. Which of these people, I ask myself, could turn into a raging torrent, or a snake, or win a hurling match single-handed or even wake a beautiful princess with a kiss that withers impenetrable hedges? Which of them can sing songs or weave words so that walls fall down?

To quote George Bernard Shaw: "How long, O Lord, how long?"

Maybe tomorrow.

Margaret Johnston

Margaret Johnston was born in Upperlands, County Londonderry on 2 May 1943. She has two sons, one daughter and six grandchildren. She started bowling short mat in 1964 and outdoor bowling in 1977. Her medal tally in World, Commonwealth and Atlantic Rim events to date are: eight gold, three silver, one bronze. With Phyllis Nolan of Blackrock Bowling Club, she holds the record of winning the World Pairs in three successive series in 1988, 1992 and 1996. She received the MBE in 1991 for services to sport in Northern Ireland.

In sport there is no Border. During the 30 years of "The Troubles", there has been no interference with any sporting body, north or south of the Border. Perhaps if all politicians were sports persons and the population were more sports-oriented, our "Troubles" might never have happened.

Nobody can choose what environment they are born into and people forget that they are only here on this earth for a short time. So, Border or no Border, none of us will take Ireland with us when we die. So why the problem?

Dennis Kennedy

Dennis Kennedy currently lectures in European integration at the Institute of European Studies at Queen's University in Belfast. From 1985 to 1991, he was Head of the European Commission office in Northern Ireland, a period which saw the reform of the EU's structural funds and the first moves to significant EU support for cross-border co-operation in Ireland. He had returned to Northern Ireland in 1985 after almost two decades in Dublin where he had been Deputy Editor of The Irish Times. *Prior to that he had worked as a journalist in Africa, North America and Belfast.*

Borders are very European things. There must be more borders per square kilometre in Europe than anywhere else. This multiple division of the western end of what geographers call the Eurasian landmass into separately governed states is what makes Europe different, and, according to some, is one of the factors that has made it such a dynamic force in world history — in science, in the arts, in exploration of, and conquest of, much of the rest of the world.

Borders are part of the European scene; they are normal. They are the lines on maps which have gradually become fixed to mark out the areas within which groups of people conduct their political affairs. These lines have not always been easily agreed. Not everyone has been too happy with where the line has been drawn. In some cases bitter wars have been fought before the line has been fixed.

But they are there because they define the approximate homelands of groups of people who identify with each other, and who want to order their affairs together. This sense of identity may have been based on a common language, or religion or other cultural dimension, or on a combination of these, or on historical circumstance, or even on convenience and mutual benefit.

Unfortunately, this evolution also gave rise to the myth of the nation, the idea that people are naturally divided into nations, and that each nation has a right to its own homeland, and a right to fight for it if necessary. So Europeans became nationalists, and Europe became as famous for its wars as for its borders, culminating in the catastrophe of the Second World War.

Since then, most Europeans have learned to live happily with their borders. European integration has not been about removing or altering those borders, but about accepting them as permanent and making them as permeable as possible; in fact, about guaranteeing that people, things, commerce, finance and almost everything else can move across them.

The Irish Border is little different from any other. It is there because the people on the island wanted and still want to order their affairs differently — a view endorsed overwhelmingly in last year's referendums. In ways, the Irish Border is the least visible and the most permeable border in Europe. Thousands of people cross it every day without being too sure exactly where it is. There is no passport or immigration control, there are no border check-points, there is no language difference, no cultural difference. With any luck, there will be no currency difference in the near future.

But it is not the same as most other European borders. It remains a disputed border. The amendments to the Republic's constitution removing the explicit territorial claim have not yet been permanently incorporated, and the revised version retains an implicit claim. More important, the Belfast Agreement cements politics in Northern Ireland along the unionist/nationalist division; that is, the Border remains, theoretically at least, the key issue. And there is still, in the island, an armed minority ready to use violence to remove the Border.

It is this threat, both real and rhetorical, to the permanence of the Border, which can make cross-border co-operation problematic. For much of the past three decades, military check-points, cratered roads and blown-up bridges made the Border both real and visible, but they were there not because there was a political boundary, but because terrorists were trying to force its removal.

So the suspicion lingers that cross-border co-operation can have a political motive, and may be more concerned with the eventual elimination of the political boundary itself than with the minimising of any negative effects its existence may have on the local economy, or inconvenience it may cause to Border-area residents.

Border areas, almost by definition, are removed from national or provincial administrative and commercial centres. Border-area residents are inevitably drawn towards those centres for education, health treatment, employment and a range of other economic, official or communal services. Looking inwards towards those centres, and not outwards across the Border, is part of the normal pattern of life.

But that "normal pattern" inevitably increases the peripherality of Border regions, with negative economic and social effects, and does nothing to promote the mutual understanding and habit of working together that are deemed essential to reconciliation and stability.

The boost to cross-border co-operation from European funding may produce some daft ideas and lead us up some cul de sacs, but it helps promote the habit of cross-border working. Such co-operation becomes a normal activity, and should help us regard the Border as "normal", as part of the scene here as elsewhere in Europe. We can then proceed to ignore it for most practical, if not political, purposes.

Sister Stanislaus Kennedy

Sister Stanislaus Kennedy, widely known as Sr Stan, is a native of Lispole, County Kerry. She joined the Sisters of Charity in 1958, and has been instrumental in developing and implementing social service programmes that have benefited thousands of needy people, particularly those who are out of home.

When talking to someone about the Border the other day, in the context of writing this piece, I found myself saying, "Of course I have visited there many times". At the time, I didn't realise what I was saying: I was identifying the Border with Northern Ireland, confusing the line on the map that divides Northern Ireland from "us" with the statelet of Northern Ireland itself. I think that slip of the tongue speaks more eloquently about my attitude to the Border — the attitude, I should say, that the Border creates in me — than anything else I can say.

That is the effect that borders have. We all erect borders around ourselves when we feel vulnerable, exposed, fearful, possessive, territorial — from garden fences to asylum walls and from ditches and hedges to political borders. They are supposed to keep us safe. We think we are keeping the enemy out. Usually, though, what we are really doing is keeping ourselves fenced in. Worse, we are creating a division that goes so deep, psychologically, that we come to see the border itself as an entity, rather than as what it is supposed to be — merely the demarcation between two real entities.

As soon as it is established, then, a border — the one that scars the map of this island as much as any other —

takes on a life and a rationale of its own. It becomes a symbol of the division and the hatred between peoples, a symbol of violence, aggression, differences, distance, distrust. More than a symbol, it becomes a stark and powerful force that itself creates enormous fear — fear whipped up through false information, lack of information, misinformation and lies, manipulated by groups thirsty for power, separating peoples and groups and creating walls of prejudice.

And yet, it is facile to think that physical borders are what divide us. The rift between North and South in this country is deep and painful, but it is as nothing compared with the rift between Catholic and Protestant inside the Border. In 1974, I took part in an ecumenical retreat in Belfast. Thirty Catholics and thirty Protestants participated. None of the Catholics had ever spoken to a Protestant before and vice versa. That is a breathtaking statistic about an island of this size. Between the two groups, there was a vast wall of prejudice, misunderstanding and ignorance. Each group lived in its own area, each had its own set of convictions and its own way of slanting information and justifying itself. The retreat was a time for breaking down barriers, but it is not easy when the barriers are not just on a map but in your own innermost heart.

Later that same year, I worked in Detroit, and there, where there are no physical borders, I experienced a similar division between communities, between the richest people living in the luxurious areas and the people living only a few roads away in a world of squalor and violence. Between these areas is a thick psychological border, whose main manifestation is fear.

This sort of economic division exists in most cities I have visited. And it is not just in cities. Other invisible borders that we erect are built to exclude the Travelling community in this country, to exclude refugees and asylum-seekers, to exclude prisoners, drug-users and the homeless. The common element in all these borders and barriers is fear of the Other. Not fear of economic disaster or even violence, though that is how we may rationalise our fear. Fear simply of the Other. Fear of people with a different way of life, a different mindset, a different set of values, a different language or accent, a different way of dressing, different social rituals, different manners.

The reason for our fear is that if we accept the Other, if we are prepared to take them on their terms, then we might lose ourselves, lose our own identity, what it is that makes us different, better, superior. The views and attitudes of the Other disturb us and sow seeds of doubt about our own natural superiority.

The Berlin Wall fell without anyone firing a single shot. It collapsed in ruins before the forces of life and liberty. Borders of fear and hatred are only weakened when trust begins to flow. And that trust depends on all of us and our belief in unity and liberty.

Our Border here will only start to fall when we recognise that we are all part of it. We either work to maintain it or we work to break it down. Leaders like David Trimble, Seamus Mallon, Gerry Adams, John Hume, Mo Mowlam are needed, but ultimately they depend on us. It is only the people who can dismantle it.

Tony Kennedy

Tony Kennedy was born in 1948. He has been Chief Executive of Co-operation Ireland since 1992. Formerly he was Regional Director of the Northern Ireland Housing Executive and Chief Housing Officer of Wakefield. He is a member of the Institute for Multi Track Diplomacy and Regional Co-ordinator for Ireland for the World Economic Forum's Transition to Peace Programme. He is a Board Member of the John Hewitt International Summer School, Ulidia Housing Association, Northern Ireland Council of the European Movement, and Civitas. He is married with three children. His nationality is British.

Jean Monnet, one of the founders of the European Coal and Steel Community, once remarked that "Borders are the scars of history on the face of Europe". Today in the European Union, after five decades of political, economic and social projects to promote integration, the scars are less vivid, though borders still exist and divide.

Throughout the Union, border areas are recognised as tending to suffer from higher unemployment and greater socio-economic disadvantage, although there are many local initiatives and Europe-wide programmes established to redress deprivation and build trust and relationships across the divides. The Border on the island of Ireland is one of many borders, though one where the scars of history remain at their most vivid.

My first contact with crossing the Border was, however, benign. Although my mother moved from Dublin to Belfast when my parents married, my grandparents lived in Dublin and we were regular visitors. Visits to Dublin were exciting treats, the accents were different, the city was more glamorous, though travelling by train, we were never quite sure where the Border was. We knew we were in the South when we crossed the bridge over the Boyne at Drogheda.

As we got older and in our teens mixed with young people living near my grandparents, differences became more apparent. In the early 1960s, there was rarely tension in this, apart from some time later when a girlfriend did not want her parents to know she was going out with a Northern Protestant. Instead there was the enjoyment of exploring different perspectives of the world, talking with friends at a time when we were forming our own world views.

That there were, and are, differences is obvious. For the half century after the Border was established, already existing divisions between North and South were increased by the government policies in both parts of the island. With membership of the European Community coming so quickly after the breakdown in civil society in Northern Ireland, and the national ambivalence of the United Kingdom towards this membership, the growth of a European identity to complement existing identities has been much less evident in Northern Ireland than in the Republic. The increased self-confidence in the South and its attraction to being a part of Europe has served to distance many of its citizens from any involvement with Northern Ireland.

This completely understandable view was exemplified by the journalist from County Cork on a Co-operation Ireland visit to Belfast who, when asked if she had been to Northern Ireland, said "No", though she had been in

Dundalk once — and she noted that they started getting different there.

In Northern Ireland, people have behaved as people do the world over when they feel under threat. Both Catholics and Protestants have retreated into their own communities and have reinforced their own identities. On Co-operation Ireland exchanges, participants expect different views to be present between Northern Protestants and Southern Catholics. There are frequent surprises when Northern and Southern Catholics discover their differences. While there are divisions in social and cultural views, reflected in part by the Border, there are also other divisions on the island of Ireland, many other less formally demarcated borders.

However, even across the political Border, the division is not always as great as is believed. At its most vivid, this is demonstrated by the shock that children from the Shankill Road in Belfast had when they discovered, on driving over the Border, that it was not demarcated by a wall in the same way that the borders of their community in Belfast were. Or the discovery of another group that the generally used language in Dublin was English, not Irish or (as some imagined) Latin!

When young people take part in exchanges, they recognise their different identities, but they also recognise cultural experiences in common, drawn from the worldwide culture of youth. Similarly, community groups recognise similar problems experienced by their communities and learn from each other ways in which these can be tackled and community confidence be built.

Where assistance is given in reaching over the Border, the results can be startling. The EU Programme for Peace and Reconciliation has shown willingness, when prompted, for cross-border links to be built. In the area of business, the idea of linkages, promoted by Co-operation Ireland and the IBEC/CBI Joint Business Council, has been enthusiastically taken up by many small businesses which have learnt the advantages of cross-border alliance and the potential of new markets.

Much still remains to be done. The Border represents real division between people on the island of Ireland, but it is only the most institutionalised example of many divisions. We are not true to ourselves if we pretend that these divisions and the Border do not exist. In recognising them, and in respecting one another's views and culture, we can work to build on our common points rather than emphasise our differences.

Avila Kilmurray

Avila Kilmurray is Director of the Northern Ireland Voluntary Trust. She was born in Dublin and has lived and worked in Northern Ireland since 1975. She is married with three children. Her voluntary involvement has been in the areas of women's issues and trade union issues. Avila is a member of the Board of the Industrial Development Board and a member of the Vital Voices Advisory Committee in Northern Ireland. She helped to conceive and establish the Northern Ireland Women's Coalition and was a member of the negotiating team that represented the Coalition in the talks that resulted in the Good Friday Peace Agreement.

A line on the map? The impatient compromise of retreating imperialism? A latter-day defensive Black Pig's Dyke? A socio-economic opportunity to smuggle cattle and condoms? The Border can be — and has been — seen as all these things, and more. Whatever the perception, it is clear that the Border has become so tightly interwoven within the Irish psyche and political culture that it is now hard to imagine the history of this island without it. Where would we be — both North and South — if we did not have something to act as a point of reference and a focus of identity, let alone a topic of controversy and conversation? We are now either Northerners or Southerners, with all the associated paraphernalia that these identities encumber us with. It is the line on the map that defines North and South, rather than geographic precision, leaving the residents of Malin Head in a state of locational complexity.

According to the historian J.C. Beckett (*The Ulster Debate*, London, Bodley Head, 1972) the irony of the Border was that nobody actually wanted it:

> "The six north-eastern counties of Ireland were grouped together and given a parliament and government of their own, not because anyone in the area wanted (let alone demanded) such an arrangement, but because the British Government thought that this was the only possible way of reconciling the rival aspirations of the two Irish parties."

The tragedy of the Border — and the state of Northern Ireland that was established within its boundaries — was that it was drawn on the basis of a sectarian headcount. In 1920, C.C. Craig, the brother of James Craig, first Prime Minister of Northern Ireland, outlined unionist reasoning for a six-county state to the House of Commons:

> "If we had a nine-county parliament, with 64 members, the unionist majority would be about three or four: but in a six-county parliament, with 52 members, the unionist majority would be about ten" (cited in *Northern Ireland: The Background to the Conflict*, ed. J. Darby, Appletree Press, 1983).

The legacy of the Border was the institutionalisation of division, albeit that aspects of economic, cultural and political differences already existed on the island. Over the past eight decades, two states developed with increasingly divergent experiences, views and structures.

For communities located along the Border itself, there was a sense of being semi-detached. The centralising administrative tendencies in both Northern Ireland and the

Republic underpinned a back-to-back development which looked towards Belfast and Dublin as the focus of power and decision-making. The stony grey fields of Monaghan, and even more of Leitrim, felt the pull of emigration, and the decline of the railway system left the only clear connection route the Dublin–Belfast rail link. Even the first motorway in Northern Ireland ended abruptly in mid-Ulster, while early gestures towards a similar infrastructure in the Republic headed in the direction of Cork. Little wonder that the Lemass–O'Neill rapprochement in the mid-1960s was stilted and embarrassed. Some years later, the break between the pound sterling and the punt sealed the psychological withdrawal that was the Southern reaction to the Northern Troubles. The Border became just that — a boundary, pockmarked by the closure of roads that the eurocrats disapproved of.

And then came the Celtic Tiger, the Good Friday Agreement and the European Union. Trans-frontier areas became all the European rage; the upgraded Belfast–Dublin train rang with mobile phones; and office space in Monaghan was at a premium. "All is changed, changed utterly", sighed Yeatsian Sligo, which even managed to get itself designated a Border region. The Good Friday Agreement marked a general acceptance of the fact that the loyalist calculation of "six into twenty-six won't go" made more political and mathematical sense than the new republican Sinn Féin formulation of "six plus twenty-six equals one", thus opening the way to a new generation of cross-border, all-Ireland institutions. Some visionaries even talked about a possible United States of Ireland.

What has, however, become a practical option is the recognition and valuing of the different experiences that the Border gave rise to. An *à la carte* sense of identity and allegiance is now more of a reality, while social and economic policies can be compared and contrasted, with models of good practice being acknowledged and adopted. Nevertheless, the way forward is not without its problems. Apart from the continuing political uncertainties, the experience of cross-border co-operation and development has been limited. Effective cross-border power-sharing and decision-making needs to be worked at rather than taken for granted. The differences that have developed over the last 80 years are deep-rooted, and have been compounded by a misguided assumption of sameness which has masked the very real barriers to co-operation. This issue needs to be addressed as a matter of urgency if cross-border institutions are to work in practice. It is also important that in their working the local is not lost amongst the macro-policy imperatives.

When Patrick Kavanagh was faced with this quandary, he wrote:

> "I inclined
> To lose my faith in Ballyrush and Gortin,
> Till Homer's ghost came whispering to my mind.
> He said I made the Illiad from such
> A local row. Gods make their own importance."

In their eagerness, Dublin and Belfast need to take into account the views from Newry, Letterkenny and Manorhamilton — let alone Belcoo and Blacklion.

And the Border — can it be a focus for synergy rather than a sentence of division? A necklace on the teddy bear rather than a collar? What is the Border? It is what we want it to be.

Maeve Kyle

Maeve Kyle was born in Kilkenny into a strong Southern Protestant family and enjoyed a liberal upbringing and education. She lived there until she married Sean Kyle in 1954 and moved to Ballymena. She has degrees in Natural Science, Education and Sports Psychology. She represented Ireland at hockey (1948–1968) and athletics in the Olympics, 1956, 1960 and 1964. She continues to coach athletics.

The Border, that strange indefinable "thing", has been a thread in the fabric of my sporting life since I was a young schoolgirl in Dublin. In the 1940s, I was lucky to be selected for a "Captain Ball" team (representing Dublin Girl Guides) to play Belfast in Belfast. We travelled by train, and we crossed the Border into a land of people who looked the same but spoke with very different accents. It was war time and we returned to Dublin, little affected by crossing the Border.

Throughout my university days in Dublin, I crossed the same Border many times — always to play sport, against Ulster, Wales, Scotland or whoever. People were the same, playing the same games, having the same problems, living very similar lives within our narrow sporting world. Then I met, fell in love with and married a man from "across the Border". Suddenly, I became aware that everything was not the same in the two present jurisdictions — separated by this indefinable "Border". Perception seemed to be more important than reality, and because I was a Southerner, I must be nationalist, Catholic, unsophisticated and poor. My background of liberal Protestant, academic middle-class was incomprehensible, even to my new family — but I was assured in many ways that I would have to think likewise or be forever a white blackbird.

Because of the "Border", I have learned — often with tears and frustrations — to accommodate and to try to understand the many strands which make up the people of this island. I believe we all have the same problems, joys and sorrows in our daily lives — the only "Border" which matters is the Border in our mind, which can be as important or as unimportant as we wish to make it.

Terence A. Larkin

Terence A. Larkin, BE, BSc (Tech.), FIEI, was born in Newry in 1924 and studied at the Abbey in Newry, University College Dublin and Sheffield University. He was CEO of Ardagh plc (now retired), Chair of the Governing Body, Dublin City University, 1982–92, and President of the Confederation of Irish Industry, 1986–88. He is currently Chair of Area Development Management (ADM) and URBAN North Dublin, and co-Chair of the ADM and Combat Poverty Agency Programme for Peace and Reconciliation.

My family's roots are in South Armagh, part of "that mysterious country where you don't know where the Border is" (to quote the writer Nuala O'Faolain). My paternal grandparents lived in Faughil Eire, near Jonesborough, and are buried just over the Border in Faughart. My maternal grandparents lived nearby at Newtowncloughoge. Their small holdings of land might have been transferred to the new Irish Free State by the Boundary Commission, post-1921, but that was not to be.

My parents settled in Newry. Growing up there in the 1920s and 1930s, I was aware that the Border permeated most aspects of our way of life. My earliest personal memory of the Border relates to the 1932 Eucharistic Congress. I was just eight years old, and I made the trip to Dublin with my family. It was an exciting day out, and I remember well that we had to stop twice at the Killeen Border posts on the main Dublin–Belfast road on both legs of the journey. This was to be a feature of all my subsequent childhood trips to Dublin.

The Border checkpoints consisted of two small huts less than half a mile apart. They had a temporary look about them: both huts were mainly of wooden construction, without the slightest sign of sophistication. They were not upgraded until the 1960s. The customs officials on the Northern side seemed then to regard their job as cosmetic, but their Southern counterparts were very officious in seeking to ensure that no prohibited goods or vehicles illegally entered the Free State.

At that time, the South was building its manufacturing base by selectively restricting imports. Accordingly, it was important for the Southern authorities to control entry through the land boundary with the North. Thus, vehicles had to be registered for cross-border movement and were provided with a triptych, similar to a passport. Vehicles were required to cross the Border on "approved" roads and have their triptych stamped "in" and "out" of the Free State, and to submit to a thorough examination to check for illegal imports. If one had to cross the Border outside normal opening hours, it was necessary to seek a "request", stating the time of one's return and paying a fee of five shillings (25 pence). I recall that, on "All Ireland" days, the queues of cars were quite lengthy going South in the morning and again returning North that evening. Commercial lorries were subjected to a more rigorous treatment — with extensive form-filling — by the Northern authorities, especially after our entry to the EU.

Scarcities of selected goods and price differentials North and South made smuggling an attractive pursuit, especially during the 1939–45 war. Tea went South and butter came North — just two examples of everyday commodities illegally traded. Of course, there were more substantial illegal transactions and prosecutions were common. I went to UCD in 1942, and the bicycle was a precious possession for a student — provided it had tyres, which were practically unavailable in the South. So on my journeys home, it was critical that I brought all the necessities to keep my bike on the road. The journey home was by train — the most reliable means of transport available at that time. Once again, one was brought face to face with the Border as the Southern customs officers came onboard at Dundalk to make their inspection and their counterparts did likewise in the North at Goraghwood station. After the war, smuggling in one form or another continued and grew.

During this period, the Irish pound was at parity with sterling, so distortions due to fluctuations in the value of the currencies did not arise. Since 1979, however, when the Irish pound severed its link to sterling, trade on either side of the Border swung between boom and bust in line with exchange rate movements. This caused serious distortions for business, especially in the Border counties. These swings, as well as the disparate investment incentives and different personal and corporate tax regimes, caused difficulties for employment in the Border area.

The Border had serious adverse economic effects on the Border towns and counties from the very start. Take my home town, Newry, as an example. Before the 1921 Treaty, Newry Canal was a busy waterway used regularly by cargo boats carrying coal to Newry for distributing South of the Border and also as far as Enniskillen and Strabane. Shipments of maize also came in through the canal to large animal feed blenders in Newry. In addition, there was also the weekly arrival of the steam packet ship which plied between Liverpool, Newry and Drogheda. With the Border, this trade gradually disappeared. Similar instances of decline in other centres on either side of the Border due to the loss of their economic hinterland can be seen.

Then came the Troubles, adding further to the decline and isolation of the Border areas. Many cross-border roads were closed for security reasons. Military, police and Garda presence — with lookout posts and security stops involving armed inspections — created a "no-go" environment which stifled social and economic development, sapped the energy of those living in the area and made outsiders reluctant to visit. The authorities on both sides of the Border were so preoccupied with security issues that, while the rest of the country enjoyed the benefits of improvements in infrastructure and accelerated economic development, the Border areas slowly deteriorated.

Since the Good Friday Agreement, a number of the factors which created this unfavourable environment are gradually disappearing. Moreover, various programmes — Peace and Reconciliation, Interreg, International Fund for Ireland, etc — are all playing their part to lift the spirit of the people. What is also required is positive discrimination towards Border areas in apportioning funds for investment in education and training, infrastructure and tourism.

Above all, the people of these areas must inform themselves of what is possible, empower themselves to decide their future and build the confidence to seek the resources to achieve their aims.

Bernadette McAliskey

Bernadette McAliskey is a Civil Rights campaigner and Human Rights activist. She is a former Westminster MP. She has three children and one grandchild. She is currently active in community development with a special emphasis on rural issues.

I grew up on the border between town and country. I preferred the country. There was more of it, more space, more elbow room, and its edges stretched to the horizon.

We had a border on the wallpaper at home. It testified to triumph over the restrictions of poverty, a tasteful focus which disguised the fact that the wallpaper didn't stretch the whole way to the ceiling. We had borders in the garden as well, marking the boundaries of family sanctuary and safety.

We children knew a song about Basil Brooke, and Basil's wife's wallpaper which mustn't have reached the ceiling either. My mother didn't approve of the song much, and thought we may have learnt it on our expeditions beyond the garden border into the estate on which we grew up. We knew another about a "lorry-load of volunteers approached a Border town". I didn't know where my sisters and I picked that one up, because my father died in 1956, but it definitely wasn't on the street where we lived.

Cookstown was a market town. We often saw lorry-loads, but as a child, I had no concrete image of what constituted a Border town.

The Border? I didn't really notice it. I knew about partition of course and the usurpation of the democratic wishes of the people of Ireland in violence and threat of violence by empire loyalists. My father educated us admirably on that issue. Partition affected my life. The Border was irrelevant to it, although I understand it was of some importance to my granny during the Second World War.

Borders are edges, boundaries, margins, exclusion zones, demarcation lines. They essentially define limitations and restrictions. I cannot and would never wish to define myself in terms of my limitations or place myself at the periphery of my own existence. That doesn't mean I do not accept the relevance of borders or the Border to others.

I do not pretend sympathy for loyal Belfast/Portadown-type Border-obsessed persons (I am trying to be civil about my end-of-century prejudices). These stalwarts couldn't find the Border in broad daylight. They've never been near it. In fact, the sight of four consecutive fields, green or otherwise, could cause an attack of agoraphobia, sending them racing for the grey emotional safety of their coloured urban kerbstones and vision-restricting walls.

I do, however, have a great deal of empathy with people who live along the Border, regardless of their allegiances.

The Border is essentially a rural phenomenon. Those who live away from it may see it only as having two sides, "our" and "theirs". Those who live alongside it know its length, its every nuance, its every bizarre twist and turn across field and river and street. It affects their personal and community life in a very central way for the simple reason that it runs right through the middle of it. Communities on either side of the Border are on the margins of their own societies, peripheral to their own centres.

This marginalisation is compounded by the fact that rural communities in any society are peripheral, and the border communities are essentially rural. Where stable nation-states meet, a distinct "border community" emerges, maximising for itself the benefits of being on the edge of two societies, a cross-border community in its own interest. Along our Border, recurring history retards, distorts and fragments this process. This Border not only separates, it divides. Those at the centre cry that the centre will not hold if the frontier line is blurred by fraternising with the external enemy, or that if the guard is lowered the uncivil outsiders will invade. The Border becomes a barricade, the Border community charged with its defence.

But border communities cannot prosper if their socio-economic and cultural existence is concentrated on protecting the national identity of the centre. If they cannot exploit their border position for their own social cohesion and economic benefit, they must attempt survival in separate peripheral and opposing half-worlds. Cross-border co-operation may be the key to community survival; the price may be perceived national treason. Holding your rural ground isn't easy along a border with as much baggage as this one has.

There are two things we can do with the Border.

One is to follow my mother's example: make it the focus of attention, turning adversity into a fashion statement. Identify and address the particular problems and potential benefits the Border poses for the rural communities who live along both sides of it and commit the resources that will make it a shared central asset rather than two peripheral deficits.

The other is to get rid of it. Which brings me back to that song about Sir Basil, the wife and the wallpaper . . . and my father's perspective — *plus ça change.*

Nell McCafferty

Nell McCafferty was born in the Bogside in 1944. She got her first job in Dublin in 1970. She moves regularly between North and South. She writes for The Sunday Tribune *and* Hot Press *magazine.*

Wrap them up behind the hedge where you can't be seen, my mother warned. The punishment, should I be caught, was never spelt out, but I already knew enough about people in uniform. My grandfather had been a policeman in Derry. My uncles were customs officers. My aunt worked in a cinema. They were always on the lookout for criminal types. However, my mother needed cheap eggs and bread. So, once a week, in the 1950s, I was given money and my father's bicycle and sent down the road to Donegal. The Border was two miles from the Bogside.

The men in uniform, on both sides, were invariably pleasant as I passed through. It was the road back that was terrifying — these guys were trained to spot smugglers. The shop was about ten metres beyond the Irish customs building. The eggs and bread were handed over in a bag. Looking carefully around to ensure that nobody spotted me, I stepped into the ditch, wrapped the eggs individually in pages from an old *Derry Journal*, placed the purchases in the schoolbag, slung it over my shoulders and cycled towards the Free State customs officers. It was always heart-stopping. They never stopped me. I never knew whether they would or not. Once I got beyond them, and into no-one's land, I would be nearly free. I knew from the movies about World War Two that men in uniform had no right to pursue me into no-one's land.

The Free State men could shoot me, of course. Even though they never carried guns — that I could see. It was always tense, cycling that hundred metres towards the customs officers in the North. And what if they stopped me? They never did. I never knew whether they would or not. Uniformed men always carried guns, of course — the policemen anyway. My grandfather always did. It was always tense, cycling past the Northern customs men (we never called them British, that I remember).

Going over the Border for the summer day-trips was an entirely different matter altogether. It was a day off from smuggling, heading on the bus to Buncrana, 14 miles away. Buncrana was sun, sea, sand and endless pleasure. There was the slight matter of buying six tickets for two mammies and ten children, and scattering the children about the bus to confuse the inspector, but if my uniformed uncle John was the conductor, we always got away with it.

Anyway, that was a problem for him and my mother and my aunt — nothing to do with me on my day off. And if they hadn't been able to swindle the fares, we'd have walked across the Border anyway. Anything to get out of Derry on a Protestant Sabbath, with everything closed and a walk up the cemetery the sole source of pleasure. We walked two miles up to Hollywell Hill — where there was neither cemetery nor closed shops, but it felt like you could do what you wanted there. At the very top of Hollywell, there was a stone man and the game was to plant a stone on top of him, just as the nationalist MP Eddie McAteer always did, and make a wish for Irish freedom, whatever that was. If Ireland was that wonderful, how come they didn't have free teeth and schools and the dole, just like the North? The women of the Free State used to ask mammy and aunt, wistfully, what else we got for free in the North?

A decade later, in the 1960s, crossing the Border really did represent a march towards freedom. Towards safety, anyway. We'd leave Derry behind — the burning buildings, the dead, the men in RUC uniform, the men in British Army uniform — and be safe and sound in Donegal within minutes. Besides, on a night out there was nowhere else to go. Derry was bad enough, but one step beyond Derry and you were into injun territory. Derry sat with its back to Donegal, its face towards Stormont; and Stormont snarled at us, the snarl heard clearly at a distance of 90 miles. From the first Civil Rights march through Derry in 1968 until the first IRA ceasefire in 1994, I never felt entirely safe in the North and there were times when it was downright dangerous.

Crossing the Border into the Republic always felt like an escape — a relief, a flight towards sanctuary, a release of tension, even though the people of the Republic might resent the implications of a Northern accent, bringing trouble down their way. I was aware of letting out a deep breath once the car passed into the North. The no-man's land theory had long since been consigned to movie fantasy: Aidan McEnespie had been shot dead, in the back, by a British soldier as he walked the neutral distance between the British and Irish Borders at Aughnacloy, County Tyrone; a Northern judge had been blown up by the IRA as he travelled between two borders at Newry.

The long straight road beyond Aughnacloy into the North was the worst stretch. It led towards a roundabout beyond which you could see Union Jacks and red, white and blue bunting hanging from the trees and houses. "If it ever does come to a civil war," a republican told me once, "you'll be a sitting duck going down that road towards the Union Jack." At the height of the Shankill Butchers' regime, I used to put a valium tablet under my tongue as I entered the North. The night of the day that the loyalist Michael Stone shot and bombed people in the republican cemetery in Belfast, I braked to a halt at Aughnacloy customs, turned back into the Republic and made a hundred mile detour all along the Border to Donegal, driving into Derry by a back road. The news broadcasts, every hour on the hour, left little choice. The function of the Border was starkly clear: North of it, there was death, South of it, there was life.

It still feels that way, at times of tension. Mostly though, with trade barriers lifted in the European Community, and freedom to transport eggs in either direction, it just means the hassle of British money in one pocket, Irish money in the other — if you can forget, which I never can, the outstanding matter of second-class citizenship under British rule in the North, first-class citizenship under home rule in the South.

Eamonn McCann

Eamonn McCann is a Civil Rights campaigner, a member of the Socialist Workers Party, the National Union of Journalists, Derry Trades Council, Amnesty International, Low Pay Unit. He is the author of War in an Irish Town, Bloody Sunday in Derry, War and Peace in Northern Ireland *and* Dear God. *He is a freelance columnist.*

In the end, it all comes down to economics. It always does.

The reason we have a Border has to do with the uneven development of capitalism in Ireland. The way to end the Border is to overthrow capitalism.

There is room for argument as to why, by the beginning of this century, the north-east had developed so differently from the rest of Ireland as to have different interests. Or, to put it more accurately, why the ruling classes had by then developed sharply different interests. It had something to do with the way tenants' rights in the north-east had allowed the accumulation of capital and, thus, eventually, the emergence of modern industry.

It had something to do, too, with the sectarian manipulation of Irish politics by British imperialism.

Whatever, Northern capital had an abiding interest in maintaining the link with Britain. British coal supplied power, British banks credit. The British Empire was the source of cheap raw materials and provided a protected market for finished goods.

The capitalists and aspirant capitalists of the rest of Ireland, contrariwise, needed nothing so much as protection *from* Britain, so that small, weak industries might prosper behind tariff walls and from state beneficence.

It was to defend their economic interests that the Protestant property-owners of the North embraced orangeism. Until Home Rule threatened, they had been above gaudy vulgarity of that sort.

The Belfast Chamber of Commerce was against Home Rule because it believed that commercial prosperity would thereby suffer lasting injury. The Northern Whig said: Our commercial and manufacturing classes are devoted to the union because they know that trade and commerce would not flourish without the union. Lords Londonderry and Hamilton declared jointly that Home Rule was menacing to the rights of property and so to order.

Their lordships appealed for the construction of a Protestant alliance to thwart this menace. Or, as the notorious bigot Rev. Henry Henderson put it: If we can stir up the religious feeling, we will have won. And they did stir up hatred, and they did win, and we taste the bitter fruit of that victory still.

Thus, Northern Ireland developed as an Orange State not because Northern Protestants are naturally inclined towards orangeism, which they are not, but because, at the crucial time, it suited the ruling class to promote orangeism, and the ideas of the ruling class everywhere become the ruling ideas in society.

Of course, this wasn't the economic divide marked by the Border which my mother had in mind when she'd send me off to dander out the Letterkenny Road on a Sunday afternoon to bring back cheap butter and Sweet Afton cigarettes. Still, she knew, and in other more subtle ways as well, that the economic was the aspect of partition most relevant to our lives.

The great contemporary political hero in our house was Bevan. My parents would say, "Thank god for Nye Bevan", because it was he who'd introduced the National Health Service. You get the same treatment as if you were the son of the Queen of England. My mother explained it to me. It was not like the Free State.

The first time I recall being aware of Southern politics was when Noel Browne crossed the floor. I remember the phrase exactly. It seemed so odd and intriguing. My father was talking with other trade unionists about the Free State Health Minister resigning from government and crossing over to the opposition after a Catholic conspiracy had prevented him bringing in a very modest measure of free health care for mothers and children. Who'd want to live down there? He and Jim Sharkey, also of the Electrical Trades Union, would agree with one another.

We knew from when we were no height that there was more to partition than national allegiance. It was the same now, too, although different.

Fight for freedom, say republicans. But how can the Bogside free itself into a society where Nelson Drive would rejoice to live, too?

Only by each lifting oppression from the other. Which is to say, only through struggling together to advance the interests we have in common. And if we do that, then, willy-nilly, we'll be struggling alongside Fatima Mansions, Ballymun and Darndale as well.

East and west of the river, North and South of the Border, we need a decent minimum wage, no tuition fees for students, an end to hospital closures, no cutbacks in education and so on and on. This is the basis for the only kind of cross-border co-operation which it makes sense for working class people to involve themselves in.

All this is self-evident, mere common sense. It is not the problem but the solution. Anybody can understand it. It is the simple truth about the Border which powerful interests, orange and green, want desperately to make seem elusive.

Felicity McCartney

Felicity McCartney was born and brought up in Lurgan, County Armagh. After graduating from Trinity College, Dublin she taught Geography in Ghana, and then returned to Belfast where she became involved in community work, first in west and east Belfast, and later in Coleraine and Limavady, working in both a paid and voluntary capacity with youth projects, women's groups and peace initiatives, to name a few. After a spell at home looking after her two children, she studied for an MA in adult and continuing education and returned to community work in Limavady Community Development Initiative in 1988. She joined the staff of Northern Ireland Voluntary Trust in 1992. Her interests include travel, drama and all kinds of music.

My early memories of the Border are having to make a day-trip to Dundalk so that we could renew our triptych, a fairly bureaucratic process involving queues at government offices in both Newry and Dundalk. In those days the Border seemed to be a barrier where people and cars were checked and where the adults became nervous about whether they were carrying anything customs officials wouldn't like.

This was in contrast to how people along the Border itself viewed it. My mother was from South Armagh and the friends and neighbours we visited there often walked across for cheap butter and some had farms which straddled the Border. They were far more relaxed about the boundary in many ways, though I was amused at the way my mother and cronies, County Armagh Protestants, talked about people from "away up in the Free State" as if it was a thousand miles away instead of only four!

Later, when I went to live in Dublin, I came to view the Border from the other direction and that was very different. There it was regarded as a complete anomaly. Dublin regarded itself as the natural centre and capital for all of Ireland, including the north-east corner variously referred to as "the black North" and "the wee North". The Border was regarded as a source of amusement and Northerners treated with the same attitude the metropolitans reserved for other "culchies". In Dublin I began to understand the great variety of customs and culture throughout Ireland. You only have to look at accents and funerals for two signs of how differences can be very localised.

Back in the North again, I came to realise that the Border had significance to people's definitions of themselves, what we now call "identity". For some, a line on a map, and for others, their very definition of themselves as being on one side or the other of that line. It was a defining factor of who we were. To quote the Beatles, "It loomed large in our legend". Crossing the Border was no big deal for me now. By that time I had travelled extensively in Europe and Africa and seen many a border, some where language, culture and political systems changed more than they ever did in a divided Ireland.

Then came the "Troubles". The Border took on a more sinister appearance, with army and police replacing the customs officials. By the time a few customs posts had been blown up, the security forces became the line on both sides. Little did we know when we were nervous of the customs officials as children that their presence was to be replaced by barbed wire, armoured cars and guns on a scale that I had encountered along the Eastern European frontiers but never imagined in Ireland. How did we ever reach the stage of people killing and defending each other in the streets and county roads? Is any line on the map worth this?

Europe has become more frontierless, more of "a uni-state but not a uni-culture". The Border never did feel like a national boundary to me and now it's like most other European frontiers. I cannot regard people in Monaghan and Louth as foreigners. When I travel around Ireland, it feels like my country as much or more than when I travel around England or Scotland. There are regional differences, yes, but these tend to be gradual rather than sudden. It is important to belong somewhere. I belong in Northern Ireland and also in Ireland, the British Isles and Europe. How would I feel if the Border wasn't there or was dramaticaly reduced in significance? I would be happy. The line on the map is not as important as the belonging people feel. It's what the Border represents for people that needs changing.

So can we sort this one out so that anybody who wants to be British AND Irish can be either or both and live on one side or other of this line without having to fight to maintain an identity? We live a sheltered life, like adolescents clinging onto a "tribal identity" and territory, self-centred and convinced that other people's views are irrational. We all need to grow up and embrace joined-up thinking. The main difficulty we have had as a community is seeing the other's point of view as valid. That is the greatest unifying factor across the divides in Ireland.

Ian McCracken

Ian McCracken was born on 30 September 1937 in Ardagh, St Johnston. He was educated in Ardagh National School, Sligo Grammar School (1951–56), Trinity College Dublin (1956–60). He taught physics in Mountjoy School (1960–61) and did a HDipEd. He worked as a physics teacher in Foyle College in Derry (1961–98) and is currently working as a Development Officer for Donegal with Derry and Raphoe Action. Ian married in 1961 and lives in Ardagh, just 100 metres from his birthplace. He is a Presbyterian.

I first became a cross-border worker in 1961 when I came to teach in Derry and lived in the foothills of Ardagh some four miles above St Johnston. My recollections of those days travelling by car are having to stop at the customs post to get the pass book stamped. This was a very im-

portant event and although there was no physical obstruction, one could not cross the Border without this ritual. It was even more important to have the return journey recorded with the customs stamp, accompanied in
each case with the duty officer's signature. The Border was
open from 8.00 a.m. to 12.00 p.m. An official crossing
outside these hours could only be obtained by making a
request. This was a statement that one would be at the
border post at a specified time. The fee for this service was
two shillings (ten pence). The system worked well. However, if going to a cross-border party, it was necessary either to be Cinderella and cross the Border before midnight
or enter a request for a later specified time. This involved
skill in estimating how good the part would be and if one
could leave at the chosen time — not always possible to
gauge accurately.

Some goods could be taken across the Border either
way, but in both cases this required completing (i) a duplicate set of papers for the Northern customs and (ii) a
different set of duplicate papers for the Southern customs.
These import/export forms were not available at the Border customs post. In my case, the Southern forms were
available in St Johnston and the Northern forms in the
Whitehouse in Derry. So the forms had to be obtained
from each source, completed and presented, with the item
being imported/exported at the respective customs posts
at the Border. Not too bad, but describe a piece of goods in
an unofficial way (e.g. an adjustable spanner as a monkey
wrench) and there could be difficulties. The Border
crossing generated some inconvenience.

Smuggling inevitably played a role in the activities of
most residents of Border areas. There abound many sto-

ries of how goods were shifted in whatever direction despite the vigilance of customs officers. In the 1950s, bathroom fittings were difficult to obtain or expensive in the Republic. A certain gentleman, of known smuggling prowess, wished to import some of these items. He put a cat in the boot and drove up to the Eire customs. On being asked to open his car boot, he showed pronounced reluctance on the grounds that he had a cat in there which was very wild and he had spent hours getting it in there. The officer insisted. The boot was opened wide. The cat took off up the road at a great rate. There was nothing for it but to return and catch the animal. An hour later, he drew up at the customs post, scratches to hands and face — all self-inflicted. "You gave me some trouble today, sir, but I have managed to recapture the beast." He passed through with his bathroom fittings packed in the boot. The Border has generated some ingenuity.

The customs posts have long since gone. Yet the Border remains. For most years of my Border-crossing experience, "Border" was synonymous with "customs". These days, excise duties still apply which the ingenuity of smugglers in fuels exploit. The difference in rates between sterling and the punt means for the cross-border worker having a purse for each — will the euro in January 2002 demand purchase of yet another purse? The influence of the Border is also experienced in the imbalance in the taxation rates between the two jurisdictions. The Border has generated some inequality.

Living, as my wife and I have done, four miles from the nearest village, and teaching in Derry, necessitated us being a two-car family. As my wife is not mechanically minded, she needed a better car — the family car. I am more interested in why a machine does not work than in either its appearance or its performance. The fact that some of my cars down the years have been the source of amusement is partly due to the above reason, but there are also economical factors. There were always adverse price differentials in car prices for the Southern resident. Yet a Northern resident can buy a normal family car new in the Republic, import it into Northern Ireland and pay in excess of £2,000 less than a resident of the Republic would pay for the same car. The Border has generated inconsistencies.

Not being a very politically active person, the presence of the Border neither excites nor annoys me. There are economic effects, but these tend, over a period of time, to level out in "swings and roundabouts". The Border has not hindered social exchange across the frontier, except perhaps for a time in the 1970s. Any decline in social activity is more related to "*sean aois*" than anything else. As a Presbyterian born, bred and educated in the Republic, I feel a strong identity with Irish culture and Celtic music and tradition. I regret the loss of the old Gaelic script and the evolution of professional Rugby Union. The Border cannot be blamed for either of these.

Mamo McDonald

Mamo McDonald is an enthusiast. The challenge of rearing a family of eleven in a difficult Border business environment has not curtailed her as a community activist, promoting women's equality and recognition of the value of older people in society. A former National President of the 39,000-strong Irish Countrywomen's Association and current Cathaoirleach of Age and Opportunity, she has in her 71st year started the Women's Studies programme at University College Dublin. To mark the dawn of the United Nations' Year for Older People, Mamo fulfilled a lifelong ambition of backpacking in Southern India.

"'Snow in May, no rent to pay'; did'ye ever hear thon spake?"

The voices behind me on the bus were strange. Gone the singsong accents of West Cork; these more clipped and Northern accents reminded me of a young bank official who had come to work with my father. At Christmas, unable to get home to Clones, he spent the holiday with us. His mother sent white bread, "smuggled across the Border," he said. More highly prized than the Christmas cake in those scarce wartime days, the bread was doled out in frugal slices. The donor became our only point of reference to "the Border".

It was a long journey from Skibbereen to my very first job in 1949 at the Hibernian Bank, Cavan. It wasn't only the strange accents I noticed but the very different landscape; drumlin country, bumpy hills pocketing small lakes and a surprise round every corner. There were other surprises.

"How much did she go for?" I heard that after a funeral. Auctioning the body? No, just the custom of funeral offerings which continued for another few decades.

More shocking was the question: "What sort is he?" or "Is she one of ours?" Strange people, I thought, noticing their reserve and guardedness.

Still, within a year I had met and married Eugene, the love of my life, and came to live in Clones with its lovely open Diamond topped by St Tiarnach's Church of Ireland. Its monastic fame behind it, along with its status as a thriving market town, by then Clones was known for the football field hosting the Ulster Final each year and the greyhound track where trial nights meant opening our drapery shop where the punters bought goods scarce North of the Border.

Domesticity and motherhood gave me little chance for involvement in the business but, on occasional forays, I gradually learned to distinguish the differences, not just in accents but in shopping strategies, between customers from Monaghan, Cavan and Fermanagh.

There were occasional excitements, brass band parades on church holidays, bridal parties hooting up the town as everyone came out to wave, herds of horses clip-clopping to the station where they were being shipped out to the Belgian Army, evangelical preachers on the Diamond with a gaggle of giggling children round them. Ulster Final day was a high point when county colours lit up the thronging streets and Northern cousins came to visit. On return visits, we would "put in requests" at the Border customs post

(I think it cost one and sixpence) for an after-hours crossing.

In 1957, there is a very clear memory of an evening when a cortege passed down Fermanagh Street. It was the mass exodus of one extended family from the town. Catching one of the last trains out of Clones station, they were getting a send-off from their friends and neighbours in Analore Street. A railway family, the closure of the Great Northern lines meant emigration for them and many others. Ever since the creation of the Border, Clones had been diminishing; the closing of the railway was a severe body blow.

When a guild of the Irish Countrywomen's Association was formed in 1959, I got the chance to meet other women, not just from the town but from Aughdrumsee, the northern part of our parish. We shared recipes and problems, knitting patterns and life stories. We went to the ICA college at An Grianan and interacted with Women's Institutes across the Border.

It was around that time that the "Troubles" started, the IRA's "Border campaign". It resulted in the spiking of roads, isolating many people who lived on the Border. My brother-in-law, Eugene McCabe, finding his direct access to Clones spiked, cut his own Khyber Pass at Kilroosky, connecting two southern lane-ways. Later, my mother came to live in the house left in the resulting triangle of land and, as it straddled the Border, she slept with her head in the South and her feet in the North.

The IRA campaign petered out and was followed by a period of relative peace. Travelling to Munster for holidays, however, we would remark on the improving roads, railways, accessibility of services and realise that we were living in a buffer zone; the Border region had become the no-man's-land between North and South.

Still we were an enterprising community, opening one of Ireland's first credit unions in 1959. Shops stayed open till ten o'clock on Saturday nights and the town had a buzz about it then. Eugene McCabe won the first Irish Life drama awards with *King of the Castle* and we would watch other plays by him on our recently acquired TV sets. We hosted an Ulster and an All-Ireland Fleadh when everybody got in on the guesthouse-keeping and catering scene.

The town, which had business equally divided between Catholic and Protestant when I first came, now became more noticeably one-sided. Protestants moved North or followed their emigrating children to make new lives in Canada.

An invitation to the ICA (now mostly Catholic, since Protestants tended to join Women's Institutes across the Border) to be involved in Women's World Day of Prayer resulted in an annual get-together, doing the circle around three churches — Presbyterian, Church of Ireland and Catholic. "Isn't it great we get the chance to meet but a pity we don't have more time to chat," one woman said as we came down the Church of Ireland steps. Next year, it was our turn, so we organised a cup of tea in the community hall beside the "far convent" chapel. The tea ceremony became part and parcel of the annual event and we got to know one another better.

The "Northern Troubles" were our troubles too; incendiary alerts provoked frantic searches, seeking out danger among the coats and suits. Horrific bomb scares at night, hauling sleeping children from their beds for the terrifying dash from house to car, then out the country for sanctuary. Some bombs did explode and without warning. One ripped apart a whole section of Fermanagh Street, did enormous damage all over the town with, amazingly, no loss of life.

Membership of the European Economic Community created a general lift and the opening of a meat factory brought new prosperity. There were stories of cattle dizzy from the "premium carousel" round and round the ring roads, picking up the grants on each circle. Business improved for a short spell and we were "*ar muin na muice*".

My Eugene's death in 1979 brought the worst tragedy for me and the children and, yet, in all the sadness and pain, there was an awareness of other layers of "family". All sections of the community grieved with us and surrounded us with love, consolation and solidarity.

That feeling of "belonging" was enhanced when, on being elected National President of the ICA, the town turned out to welcome me home. The status of "blow-in" behind me now, I truly was a Clones woman.

The closure of the Border roads (especially Lackey Bridge which connected our parish) in the early 1980s caused the "death" of the town. With two-thirds of our hinterland in Fermanagh and 75 per cent of our business coming across the Border, in one short week we lost all that and survival for the business community became a never-ending struggle.

"Poor Clones" we heard and, as the town declined, we watched others prosper. The European philosophy of free access of people, goods and services between member states rang very hollow in our ears. At one period, there was sexual harassment by British soldiers of women living on one side of the Border but working on the other, a very powerful disincentive to crossing at all. There was, all during this time, a marked disinclination at Government level in Dublin to listen to our problems, let alone address them. A delegation to one Minister was told: "Ah, sure, don't tell me about Border troubles. Don't I come from a border myself, between Limerick and Kerry!"

Still, amidst the worry and gloom, we gloried in the triumphs of our Clones Cyclone, Barry McGuigan, and later the success of Pat McCabe with his *Butcher Boy*. A small study group identified the needs of Clones, backed up by research and a local survey. The idea for Ireland's first National Garden Festival was born. Sold at organised fireside meetings in every street and out the country, there was strong support in the area. We formed a development co-op and before long gathered sizeable funds and, though we failed to get the necessary State backing for the grand plan, the funds served as priming for elements of it, supported by the Ireland Fund and Europe. The derelict Ulster Canal Stores was bought and restored, serving as a centre for arts and tourism development. The fast-fading tradition of Clones lace-making was revived and fostered. Clones Credit Union cut its annual dividend, enabling the setting-up of a local enterprise centre. The paving and refurbishing of The Diamond transformed the streetscape.

During this period I started tea-rooms within the shop, opened a small lace gallery and gradually eased out of the drapery. The teashop became the venue for early Saturday morning meetings of the development committee and the arrival point for "possible" funders — on the premise that tea, scones and apple pie could be effective "softener-uppers".

Three years ago, we sold the shop and I now live outside the town in Roslea parish. But the ties with Clones are strong and enduring; shopping, ICA and lace meetings, the church choir, events in the Canal Stores all draw me back, as well as family and friends.

Now, 50 years on, the strange has become the familiar and I now realise that the line called "the Border" has never been a boundary through the Ulster community where I live. Yet, when it has been forced upon us, it has divided neighbour from neighbour.

Reading my son Darach's novel, *The Sons of Levi*, has given me an understanding of the betrayal felt by Protestants when isolated in the "Southern" Ulster counties in 1921. We have all felt that same sense of being "forgotten people" by the neglect of successive governments, being "counted out", expendable. Our social, cultural and economic ties straddle the Border in this community and we can only pray that, with the peace process, our political ties will catch up.

This is now my place and these are now my people. Thomas D'Arcy McGee summed it up for me in his poem, *The Man from the North*.

> I wish that in Munster they only knew
> The kind, kind neighbours I came unto,
> Small hate or scorn would ever be
> Between the south and the north country.

Geoff MacEnroe

Geoff MacEnroe was appointed Director of the Irish Business and Employers Confederation / Confederation of British Industry Trade and Business Development Programme when it was launched in 1992. He previously worked with an international firm of engineers and contractors and with the Irish Trade Board where he held senior positions in Dublin, Brussels and Tokyo. He holds degrees in Mechanical Engineering and in Economics and Politics from University College Dublin.

The Border between Northern Ireland and the Republic of Ireland is a physical and psychological barrier which has limited the development of trade, business development and economic co-operation between the business communities in Northern Ireland and the Republic of Ireland. Due to the presence of the Border, the economies on either side have developed separately. The economies on both sides have suffered from the failure to develop an island of Ireland economy. It is only in recent years that major efforts have been made to identify opportunities for extending North/South economic co-operation.

Barriers Emanating from the Border

When the IBEC/CBI Trade and Business Programme was established in 1992, apart from political and security concerns, there were many real and perceived barriers to trade. Long delays for trucks at the Border inhibited the development of trade, as did the poor quality of the road and railway systems. Currency variations and different VAT and excise duties created uncertainties and price disparities. Perhaps of greatest importance was the psychological barrier caused by lack of communications.

Cross-Border Trade

Developing trade across the Border is an opportunity for a company to extend the size of the traditional home market before developing new markets which are more difficult to service. For many smaller companies, the market across the Border should be seen as a "test market", where exporters can gain experience and meet their key competitors before entering the market in Great Britain.

Companies servicing only the Southern Irish market have the potential to add an additional 540,000 households (an increase of 45 per cent) by including the Northern Ireland market. Northern Ireland companies have the potential to add an additional 1,200,000 households (2.2 times the Northern Ireland market) by targeting the Republic of Ireland market.

Industrial buyers in the South (excluding the food sector) spend over IR£7 billion a year on materials. Less than one-third of this business is placed with local suppliers.

The public sector market on the island of Ireland is estimated to be worth more than IR£6.3 billion per annum.

The level of goodwill existing on both sides of the Border towards promoting cross-border programmes aimed at developing the peace process should not be underestimated.

North/South Balance of Trade

The Republic of Ireland has consistently recorded a trade surplus with Northern Ireland. While it is concluded that there is considerable scope for increasing trade in both directions, given the size of the two economies in GDP and population terms and the structure of the two economies, there is greater scope for Northern Ireland companies to increase exports to the Republic.

Cross-Border Co-operation
Most organisations thinking of developing cross-Border contact define this in terms of exporting to the cross-Border market. It is also important to consider opportunities for developing co-operation with a partner located on the other side of the Border. The following are some examples:

- **Cross-Border Employment**. Companies located in the six southern Border counties have experienced difficulty in recruiting skilled labour locally. The EURES Cross-Border Partnerships has been established to assist employers wishing to recruit workers living across the Border. Specialist advisers on labour mobility issues have been located in FÁS offices and Training and Employment Agency job centres on both sides of the Border. These agencies have also agreed to link their IT job-brokering systems in order to exchange job vacancies automatically on a cross-border basis.

- **Co-operation for Overseas Work**. Irish companies can overcome their lack of scale by entering joint ventures with other companies. Over the past 20 years, a number of large projects overseas have been completed on a joint venture basis involving Northern and Southern companies. There is scope for expanding this type of co-operation.

- **University–Industry Collaboration**. The Conference of University Rectors in Ireland, which comprises representation from the nine universities on the island of Ireland, are working together to increase awareness of knowledge created in the universities to improve or develop new products and services. To maintain their relevance, the universities are anxious to meet the needs of industry on an all-island basis.

Providing Information on an All-Island Basis

The lack of market information, including information on the structure of industry and potential customers across the Border, is a major reason why cross-Border trade has been low and many companies do not target the market across the Border. There is a need to be able to access information on an all-island basis.

Companies North and South are being encouraged to start developing e-business, which is the process of conducting any aspect of business relationships with suppliers, customers and other business partners over the Internet. Smaller companies can achieve a competitive advantage by using the Internet.

A company in Northern Ireland has launched the first web site in Ireland providing access to the latest public sector tenders issued North and South of the Border. The "Tenders Ireland" web site will encourage more companies to target the public sector market on an all-island basis.

Remaining Barriers

The fact that Northern Ireland is outside of the Eurozone and the fluctuating exchange rate between sterling and the Irish pound remind us that the Border is a barrier that will continue to affect the maximisation of economic co-operation between Northern Ireland and the Republic of Ireland.

Ann McGeeney

Ann McGeeney was born and reared close to Crossma-glen, south Armagh. She is Joint Manager of Area Development Management and the Combat Poverty Agency in the Peace and Reconciliation Programme in the Border counties of Ireland. Prior to this she has worked in community development in south Armagh. In 1986, she helped establish the Slieve Gullion View, *a community newspaper which won the Christopher Ewart-Biggs Award. She is a member of the Northern Ireland Rural Community Network, BBC Children in Need Local Appeals Committee and works in a voluntary capacity with the Barrow Cadbury Trust in the Armagh area. She is married to Jimmy Murray and has three small children Daisy, Holly and Ardal.*

Cornonagh is what you could describe as a small peninsula townland, belonging to south Armagh but jutting into County Louth. What appears to the casual outsider as windy loanens (or lanes) leading to the middle of nowhere are in fact intricate networks of roads crisscrossing the borderland. This is where many generations of my family have farmed the land and lived the border life.

From the head to the shoulders
Right down to the spine
Was cut off old Ireland
By the new borderline . . .
— *Anon, supplied by Pete Lenaghan, Clarnagh*
and Mickey Treanor, Cornonagh

Such was the thinking of people in south Armagh in the aftermath of partition that some locals reflected in poetry. However, in the 1930s the Border provided many opportunities to turn an extra crust by way of smuggling. This was a particular feature of the war years when provisions were rationed and whilst most of the stories and poems which abound today are of the heroic battle of wits between the customs men and the smuggler men, women too played their role, often in a quiet, unassuming way.

It started with Big Annie, the grandmother, who shifted the butter and eggs to Dundalk on her bike every Monday to the street fair. Across the Border in the Free State, there were opportunities to do deals to her advantage. Her children, 12 of them, would eagerly await her return on the promise of something exotic — like a tomato or even an orange. But rarely did such luxuries cross the kitchen table; times were too hard.

When the war ended and trade favoured the movement of the eggs in the other direction — from the Free State to the North, Big Annie sent her daughters on missions of mercy to oblige an ageing cousin. Catherine and Nan, the two lassies, went down the "spout", up across the fields by the Blackstream to the isolated farmhouse on the other side. On the way, the pair scared the lives out of themselves with stories of what the customs men would do with them if they were caught.

It was in the early 1970s when to while away winter nights (not having electricity, never mind television) my mother entertained us with stories of the *craic* on the Border. We as children had no real understanding of what possible dangers my aunts had been exposed to in those "good old days", nor indeed did we really understand what the Border was about. We didn't have long to wait.

As children, we all worked hard on the farm. In the summer, we helped bring in the hay and the harvest — and the reward, the spin home on the high load of hay from one of the out-farms. We were easily amused, pulling leaves off the trees, shouting down at neighbours as the trailer wobbled over the rickety roads. On one such occasion, we were high up on the trailer when a speeding car full of dark men squealed to a stop in front of us. A gun peered out of the window and my father was ordered to move the tractor out of the way. With a lot to do, he managed to shift the load into the ditch so that the car was able to squeeze past. Having a bird's-eye view of such a scene was bewildering — the sheer panic of Daddy below getting the load, including us, out of the way. We later learned of the attack on the barracks in Crossmaglen and obviously we had been met on the escape route across the Border. And thus one of my first personal and tangible experiences of the Border was a sinister one.

This was but one of the many memories of the Border for me as a young girl. There were the pig smugglers of the 1970s when the double-trailered, multi-tiered pig transporters were regular travellers along Cornonagh road. On our way from the school bus, we were lucky to survive the illicit traffic on roads made for horses and carts, not swollen lorries.

Border life took on a different meaning for us as teenagers. Going out in the North was a risky business. She-
lagh Carnival became the focus of our social scene and this
was followed by Saturday night excursions to anywhere
from Dundalk to 'Blayney to Carrickmacross — so long as
Horslips were playing. To us life was free and easy across
the Border. The road crossings in those days were one
huge pothole — a result of the two administrations turning
their back on a shared problem — almost afraid of touch-
ing each other for fear of catching whatever the other one
had.

Teenage romance across the Border seemed like hard
work in what were troubled and dark times, but today
working life on the Border has also set its challenges. Experience of working with the communities in the Border
area has opened up new dimensions, possibilities and
sometimes the proverbial can of worms. Ways of working
are different; we operate to different legislations, like the
Roman God Janus looking towards both Dublin and Belfast, but we have made a start in moving round to face
each other through our cultural, business and community
activities. We know that there are new opportunities,
which find us travelling along state-of-the-art cross-
border superhighways and not sneaking down the windy
"spout" in the dead of night, like Big Annie and her lassies.

By the way — does anyone need a dozen eggs?

Aideen McGinley

Aideen McGinley is Chief Executive of Fermanagh District Council and was formerly Director of Development. She worked as a Planner with Donegal County Council, as a Community Services officer for Fermanagh District Council and subsequently for 13 years with Strabane District Council during which time she graduated with an MSc in Social Policy, Administration and Planning from the University of Ulster. In 1998 she received an Honorary Doctorate for her services to the community by the University of Ulster. Aideen is extensively involved in community and public bodies. She is married with three children and lives in Enniskillen.

Chocolate was always nicer in the South. As someone who has lived and worked all my life on the Border, with the exception of three years at University in England, it was the simple things like that, that stay with me. As the daughter of a vet, a sick cow in the North was the same as in the South until the day came when the drugs in the boot had to be kept separate. The bombs and bullets of the late 1970s were a dramatic backdrop as I grew up in the shadow of the Army Checkpoint with memories, some funny and too many sad.

I have worked both sides of the Border, experienced the complexities of tax and different legislative and administrative regimes, all of which underlined that imaginary line on the map and made co-operative working difficult. People fled in fear from their home place, infrastructure such as the railways disappeared and the social isolation within and between communities was re-emphasised; yet the Donegal accent is Northern and Northerners are Irish when abroad. The North used to be the place with no potholes and cheaper petrol — we are now looking enviously across the line at the impact of the Celtic Tiger or maybe, more accurately, in the Border region, the Celtic Tabby.

There are many fine examples of how we can and have worked effectively together to address our mutual disadvantage of always being on the edge of everything. Technology removes the tyrant of location and we are harnessing it. People dismiss negative prejudices and perceptions through contact such as Cross Connect between schools in Fermanagh, Leitrim and Cavan, the Wider Horizons Programme and Women's Work. Examples of hope transcend our cultural, economic and community needs. They include projects such as Scottish Opera, who in 1997 linked the communities of Garrison and Kiltyclogher — eight miles apart, yet for 25 years, as a result of closed roads, a 25-mile round trip. They created an opera on the "Ballroom of Romance" — a shared and treasured part of local history. The performance was unforgettable, or in local parlance "mighty", the audience meeting the grandchildren of their friends for the first time, in some cases, in 50 years.

The Shannon-Erne waterway has physically linked North and South and regenerated and revitalised a Border area, with tourism generating over £7 million per annum from Europe's longest navigational waterway.

The work of the cross-border local authority networks is another fine example. Co-operative action working on the ground with over one million people being represented by 17 local authorities making their voices collectively heard in the development of the first integrated Border corridor strategy in Ireland.

There are so many things we share:

- Physically and geographically we are linked
- Individually and collectively we are linked and always have been.

We must rebuild the trust and recognise that what we do must be natural, once again — not artificial or forced. It is not a game of winners and losers; it is life. And the iced caramels are good too!

Paddy McGinn

Paddy McGinn was born in Aughnacloy, County Tyrone, and educated at Queen's University, Belfast, in Agricultural Science. Since 1988, he has worked in the Republic as a Trainer and Project Manager. Working mainly with the community/voluntary sector and social partners, he has worked in the fields of Agriculture and Rural Development, Youth Work, Community and Enterprise Development. He is currently working in the Border counties as Joint Manager of the Peace and Reconciliation Programme 1995–1999, delivered by Area Development Management Ltd. and the Combat Poverty Agency.

The Border: What does it mean to me? This question evokes much sentiment and emotion from memories both good and bad. As a sixties "child of the Border", I have returned to work and live here where I was born. The Border has been part and parcel of my life, and still is.

First and foremost, the Border is an area; it's where I'm from. It is my identity. Despite the physical barriers of road closures and the checkpoint at Aughnacloy, our community had close associations with our neighbours in adjacent communities across the Border. The reason for this association is complex; however, one major contributor was undoubtedly the family ties that existed. The formation of the Border actually divided the local parish of Truagh. Families, friends, neighbours and farms were separated by the Border. Some people had to travel round trips of up to ten miles to attend their parish church, and visit neighbours and relatives; however, unapproved shortcuts were often found. This "Border area" was unique, a buffer zone, where social, cultural and economic activity often defied the boundary.

I was brought up on a staple diet of stories and family folklore of smuggling feats across the Border. Everyone was involved: Catholic, Protestant and clergyman. Merchandise from livestock to eggs to cigarettes were constantly on the move across the Border. The stories were never clear as to what direction the contraband was moving, or indeed what monetary gain would be achieved. However, major risks were always taken, whether it was for a couple of packets of cigarettes, or a vanload of pigs. The customs and police were usually involved, and outwitted on most occasions; the colourful characters portrayed were always from a local family lineage; and the storyteller never questioned the morality or legality of the operation. This mystical portrayal of smuggling was in-dulged in so often at wakes and family gatherings that I often felt envious of such fun times crossing the Border.

Other childhood memories are not so pleasant. My father, a livestock haulier, transported cattle throughout Ireland. As young children, most nights we prayed for his safe return, and hoped he would not be delayed at the Border. Often he was, reaching the Border after it had closed for the night. Sometimes he would sleep there until morning. Other times, a late-night phonecall would summon my mother to go to meet him. He would abandon his lorry and cross on foot, returning to complete his journey in the morning.

Sometimes I was permitted to accompany him on such journeys, and I remember clearly the queues of vehicles at the customs post. Papers had to be signed and stamped, checked and checked again. My father worried about the delay and feared that he might be turned back. My big days out could not be enjoyed until we had cleared customs. The return journeys were worse! Anxiety increased as the Border approached. The Southern customs "assumed you were guilty until proven innocent" according to my father. In contrast, their Northern counterparts were "gentlemen", a beatification only bestowed on them when compared to their Southern neighbours.

The implementation of the European Free Market ensured the removal of the customs. Although too late for my father's cattle haulage days, it was generally welcomed by the people of "the Border area". However, there were negative side effects. As well as direct job losses to custom officials, trade in the town was adversely affected. Smuggling, however, continued as those operating in the black economy found new money-making schemes. An important facet of the identity of this Border area was to be maintained.

The removal of the customs posts increased the significance of the Army checkpoint at Aughnacloy as the demarcation of the Border. I don't remember the crossing without the checkpoint. Although the North/South boundary was a mile away at Moybridge on the River Blackwater. you didn't feel you had crossed the Border until you negotiated the checkpoint. As I grew up, the checkpoint grew too! Fortifications increased, with bollards, ramps and barbwire being added. By the early 1980s, it had three sophisticated lookout towers, and a huge drive-through shed, where searches were performed.

Like most people, I had reason to cross the Border often. Delays were not uncommon, and occasionally you would be selected for interrogation. However frustrating at the time, this was accepted as part and parcel of living on the Border.

My earliest memories of crossing the checkpoint were exciting. On excursion from primary school, we were sometimes marched through in pairs, as we went on nature walks or to a sports day in the local playing fields. It didn't scare us; just one of the novelties on our short journey. The novelty soon wore off as I grew a little older. As young teenagers, we would cross over on our way to the pitch of our local football club, Aghaloo. To avoid the checkpoint, our parents would drop us off to walk across. However, unlike our primary school excursions, we were now sometimes subjected to questioning. Occasionally, our bags would be searched, and the brief interrogation could be frightening. On other days, the soldiers were very chatty and wanted to engage in polite banter. Our response was usually curtailed, probably wary of this "Jekyll and Hyde" syndrome, or conscious of peers, who didn't approve of friendly engagement.

When older, I once decided to drive through the checkpoint. There was no queue of traffic and I was already late for an important engagement. To my horror, I was directed into the shed. I cursed the decision I made. The doors were closed and my car was thoroughly searched. I stood there annoyed, frustrated, waiting to be interrogated. My thoughts drifted, why me? Is this a random search, a form of harassment, or have I been singled out for some reason? I remembered how my father hated the customs, "guilty until proven innocent," he said, I empathised, and at that moment, I hated the soldiers.

One Sunday afternoon, a teammate, Aidan McAnespie, crossed the checkpoint on foot, passing a long queue of vehicles, on his way to the football pitch. Aidan never got there. Shots rang out from a lookout tower and Aidan lay dead in a pool of blood 200 yards from the checkpoint. As the realisation of what had happened unfolded, the initial shock of a whole community turned to anger and disgust to disbelief and helplessness. The horror of that day will never be forgotten; it affected us all in different ways. When asked what the Border means to me, the emotions caused by that event immediately spring to mind.

The checkpoint at Aughnacloy was demolished by 1998 as part of the ongoing peace process and scaling down of border security. This was an emotional event for the people of Aughnacloy and the parish of Aghaloo. For me, the checkpoint at Aughnacloy will always be synonymous with the shooting of Aidan McAnespie, a teammate and a friend.

"My Border", the checkpoint, is gone, but the "Border area" as an identity remains, as do the memories and emotions of the people. Similar emotions exist across the religious divide right along the Border. With the help of the peace process and the Peace and Reconciliation Programme, let's hope one day we can relive the fun times crossing the Border.

Justice Catherine McGuinness

Justice Catherine McGuinness is a judge of the Irish High Court. She chaired the Forum for Peace and Reconciliation, which sat from 1994 to 1996. She has three children and four grandchildren.

For me the Border has always been important, yet unimportant. It was always there and I crossed and re-crossed it regularly, yet it had surprisingly little impact on my life. Psychologists tell us that our deeply felt attitudes and beliefs are formed in childhood and when I began to think of what the Border has meant to me, I realised how true this was. So, to try to explain what the Border was and is to me, I think I must go back to my childhood.

Dunmurry was a village then and there was countryside between it and Belfast, and more countryside between it and Belfast. It was, let's face it, a totally Protestant village, originally based on the linen industry. It was in the main a working-class village. My school-friends left home early to work in the suiting factory or the Lilliput

Laundry. My father was the Church of Ireland rector. I suppose unionism was simply assumed as the normal way of life; certainly the male culture (apart from sport) centred around the local Orange Hall, and the summer nights were sometimes loud with the Lambeg drumming competitions. On the wall of the church was the long list of parishioners who had died in the Battle of the Somme.

Since we lay on the route from Belfast to Hillsborough Castle, where the Governor lived, visiting royal personages tended to pass through Dunmurry; they did not, of course, stop. The local people turned out in fairly moderate numbers to have a gawk at them and to give them a royal cheer. We hardly ever had elections; unionist unopposed was the order of the day. Sometimes a daring red or green candidate stuck his head above the parapet, but he never had a realistic chance of election. As a result, the local MP had no need to serve his constituents through "clinics"; those sort of things were usually done by the clergy. Ordinary people saw themselves as British and "Ulster is British" was proclaimed on the wall of Glengall Street, but there was that denial of Irishness that I often find now in that community. Irishness was not political; it arose from living on this island. The Border was a fact of life, not a shibboleth, nor a war cry.

I was a child, and neither the Border nor unionist politics were part of my family. My father came from West Clare and my mother from Tullamore. My mother's two brothers were also Church of Ireland clergy working in the North; otherwise, my extended family lived in what my school-friends called the Free State. Regularly we went to stay with my grandmother in Dublin and the whole area of Rathmines is fixed indelibly in my memory as the scene of childhood walks, my mother pushing my younger brother in the pram. We went to Dublin on the train from the old Great Victoria Street Station, so much more impressive than Belfast Central. Uncles, aunts and cousins lived in Dublin or in the country near Mountmellick. We visited them and stayed with them; this was our family and their lifestyle was part of ours. The Border meant the customs men who got on our train at Goraghwood and got off again at Dundalk. During the war and post-war years, the days of shortages and rationing, my mother and my grandmother worked a co-operative system. We came to Dublin with tea, soap and white bread; we took home meat and butter. This harmless barter was not considered to be smuggling.

Later I went to boarding school in Dublin, to Clergy Daughters' School, which was attached to Alexandra College. We Northern clergy daughters, and there was quite a number of us, would meet in Great Victoria Street, our parents seeing us off with our school trunks, which travelled in the guard's van with caged (and sometimes uncaged) greyhounds and the odd basket of homing pigeons. We crossed the Border but it was impossible to see where it really was and I don't think we cared much. At the Boyne viaduct, we tried to fire pennies into the river through the girders of the bridge. It was surprisingly difficult, and I'm afraid it had nothing to do with the symbolic importance of the Boyne!

Quite a large proportion of Clergy Daughters' School pupils came from the North and we were conscious of "keeping our end up". But it had more to do with solidarity than politics. I had no sense of being in a "foreign" country; nor, I think, had my Northern companions. After all, our fathers were clergy of the Church of Ireland, which belonged on both sides of the Border. We all looked forward to the week of the General Synod in May each year, when our parents would come to Dublin and be able to visit us and take us out.

How little we knew, you will say, and what a sheltered existence we led! And you'd be right. We were cut off from the other community in the North. In the abstract we knew, as we grew up, about conflict, discrimination and hatred, but it did not greatly touch our lives. Our prejudices were polite prejudices. Yet, I think, it would be a mistake to overlook the existence within the Protestant community of a sizeable group of people (who were by no means all the children of the clergy) who ignored the Border and sent their children to be educated in Dublin, both as schoolchildren and later among the considerable cohort of Northern students at Trinity. For me, it laid the foundations of a life where I have always crossed and re-crossed the Border and maintained family and friends on both sides, physically and politically.

What I have written here is neither philosophical nor political. It is not an analysis of the effect of the Border on recent Irish history. It is just a personal reflection, but I hope it may go some way to explain that we cannot all fit into neatly defined boxes with neatly defined labels. Or perhaps my particular box might be labelled "cross-border body"?

Frank McGuinness

Frank McGuinness is a playwright. He was born in Buncrana, County Donegal. He now lives in Dublin and lectures in English at UCD.

I grew up ten miles from the Border in the town of Buncrana, County Donegal. Once I was invited by a friend to talk to primary students at the Dalkey School Project. Not having kids myself, I was terrified at the audience of more than a hundred who faced me. I've spoken to a conference of psychiatrists, I've even plunged myself into a debate with a couple of theatre critics, but this was genuinely frightening. I knew that I would get away with nothing here, so I did a dangerous thing for any writer. I decided to tell the truth.

Pointing to the map of Ireland on the classroom wall, I explained my problem to them. Where was I from? Where did I live? Buncrana, and County Donegal itself, were in the North, but they were referred to as being in the South. Where did I belong? It could not be said to be up there, but it was also not down here. Neither geography nor history could really answer my questions.

One student suddenly provided the solution. He said, "You live in no-man's-land." We all agreed he was right. Since then I have been proved to be a citizen of no-man's-land, and I recognise any Border that lets me live there.

Susan McKay

*Susan McKay was born in Derry. She is a journalist with
the Sunday Tribune. She is the author of* Sophia's Story, *a
biography of child abuse survivor Sophia McColgan, and
of a forthcoming book about Northern Ireland Protestants entitled* An Unsettled People, *to be published in
February 2000.*

I come from a Border city that doesn't even have a name.
Not a name that all of us can say, anyway. Derry, Londonderry; Derry, where some of us live, shadows Londonderry, where the rest of us live. And Londonderry likewise
hovers over Derry. The town is in a state that has no
name. No name that all of us can agree, that is. But it has a
shape. A child's comfort blanket shape, with a raggedy
hole called Lough Neagh in the middle. We can all hug it
and bawl.

You see the shape on the weather maps. It will be
raining on our small island. Our Southern coast has little
headlands and inlets, and it's only when you try to go
there that you find there is no sea, just another field, and
another on beyond that. It isn't an island after all. But the
Border is there alright, an invisible crack jittering across
the country. Three hundred miles long and no one knows
how deep.

Border people are watchful. At the same time, they are
experts at turning the blind eye. Their talk tends to be
evasive. The Border turns you into what you are — a Protestant, a Catholic, a soldier of one kind or another, a
stranger. Best to stick with your own kind. If you have any.
Along its loneliest stretches you feel you are being

watched. British Army watchtowers, camouflaged like monster beetles, are vacant now. But you wouldn't be surprised, late at night, if the barrier slowly lowered and the red lights flashed.

The dragon's teeth have been pulled, or tipped to the side on roads that had quietly gone to meadowsweet and grass in the years they were closed. Stone arches of old bridges bombed in the 1970s have been left to decline gracefully, recently replaced by efficient concrete. Brash new EU highways find their way into little towns in the Republic that seem to have been asleep since the 1950s. Bars with wooden counters and shoes for sale. Potholes on Main Street. A Fermanagh man was asked in Cavan was he from Scotland.

Border towns have a restless feel. The frontier won't settle. Nationalists don't want it to. Derry is pushing towards the hills of Donegal. Dundalk waits its moment to move back North. The air is thin in the places that used, when there were customs posts, to be called no-man's-land. A certain sort of establishment flourishes. Bars that feel like last-ditch saloons, their customers alert for the moment when the doors swing inwards. Lurid pink hotels with parking for a thousand trucks.

Fortunes are made and lost. A big house rears up beside an imposing redbrick garage, but before it's finished, the cars start going the other way to some man with a tank of diesel and a hand-painted sign on the other side. Punts and pounds. Much furtive business is done in lay-bys, watched by grave-eyed sheep and cows in trailers. The animals, according to the painter Dermot Seymour, know that there is no such thing as history here. Wherever that is. It is mysterious, the Border.

There are fields abandoned by Protestant farmers too scared by the IRA to stay, too bitter to let go the land, Badlands where strenuous ragwort boasts its garish yellow victory. Patrick Kavanagh's black hills look North at them. Unapproved roads where bodies were dumped. Sometimes a rosebush to mark the spot. Often not. There are nationalist towns stranded on the wrong side when the Border was drawn around them. Sullen and failing to thrive in a unionist state whose leaders said the Catholic people were disloyal.

Paisley's deputy paced the Border with a measuring tape, ready to cost a Chinese wall. "We will never exchange the blue skies of Ulster for the grey skies of an Irish Republic." Loyalist graffiti. In Pettigo, the statue of an IRA man points his gun across the Termon River into Tullyhommon. Pettigo is in Donegal and Tullyhomman is in Fermanagh. Before partition, the two villages were one.

The poet Padraic Fiacc wrote, "These civil wars are only ever over on paper." Of course, most people just go about their business. As we say. Passing no remarks. And, in towns and villages all along the Border, the hanging baskets, full of Peace and Reconciliation flowers, look nice, swinging in the wind that blows both ways.

Tommy McKearney

Tommy McKearney is a former political prisoner, was reared in the County Tyrone village of The Moy, and was educated in St Patrick's Academy, Dungannon. He now lives in County Monaghan and is currently employed by EXPAC (Ex-Prisoners Assistance Committee). EXPAC is one of the many projects supported by the Special Support Programme for Peace and Reconciliation.

Some people seem not to know even the most basic pieces of information. This fact struck me clearly one day in H-Block Six when I asked a fellow republican prisoner if he had heard any news.

A hijacking had occurred, he told me, somewhere on the Border. I asked him where exactly this had happened. He said that it was near one of those Border towns — Newry, Donegal or Cookstown or some such place. His determination to get rid of partition certainly seemed greater than his understanding of its whereabouts.

We shouldn't be too severe on the lad though. He was too young to have had the opportunity for much travel or education. The same excuse could hardly apply to the ITN News reporter who once told of an IRA landmine attack near Dungannon. The culprits, according to him, had detonated the bomb by command wire from their hideout in nearby Eire.

Such ignorance has always come as something of a surprise to me. While I was being reared in County Armagh in the 1950s, my County Roscommon born mother's family still lived in rural countryside, west of the Shannon River. Every summer we crossed the Border and visited our relatives. The road through Middletown, Tyholland and on to Monaghan was as familiar to me as the road to Blackwatertown, Killyman or Benburb.

Indeed, one of my earliest memories involves just such a Border crossing. We were travelling after dark in my parent's old Ford Prefect van. We were tired children and becoming increasingly irritable. To make matters worse, the infant had lost his "dummy" under the seat. Few vehicles had interior lights in those days, so Mother couldn't see to retrieve the baby's soother.

The situation improved through unlikely circumstances. We were stopped by a B-Special patrol and my father persuaded the "Specials" to loan us a torch. Mother found the "dummy" and some calm returned. It was a number of years before I was to realise that, as well as assisting travellers, B-Specials along the Border had other responsibilities.

Such innocence could not have lasted. Learning of the Border's wider significance didn't take long. Not, however, as some of those who know me now might suspect. My education came through dubious practice nevertheless.

In my early teens, two elderly great uncles employed me as an apprentice "bag-man". I was tasked, that is, to accompany them to cockfights — usually on the very line of the Border — carrying their prize bird in an old hemp sack.

My real value to the great uncles was my ability to run effortlessly for hours. We could therefore exploit the differing jurisdictions whenever we were forced hastily and prematurely to abandon a contest. There are strange ways to learn the idiosyncrasies of international boundaries, but fleeing breathlessly from the Gardaí with a rooster under your arm while looking desperately for sight of a red post-box has got to be one of the oddest.

Time passed and things changed. I didn't know Middletown so much for its proximity to Long Nancy's but for its grim and worrying military fortification. For us republicans, the political entity we disliked so deeply seemed to take on a suitably sinister and ugly appearance. Moreover, since the Border was in essence the first line of defence for the Northern security apparatus, it was also a place where many of us endured the closest attention from the British Army.

In recent times, that aspect of the Border has greatly changed. Almost all of the checkpoints have been dismantled and late-night journeys are no longer the same discomfort. There are all the signs of returning to normality.

Yet there remains the very real difficulties caused by different currencies, unequal and distorted economic development, differing social legislation and a host of minor irritants, such as knowing whether to count journeys in miles or kilometres.

Many won't agree with me, but it still seems an awful pity to me to see the Border cause these divergences when I just can't see that many differences between the people I grew up with in County Armagh and the people I now live among in County Monaghan.

Martin Mansergh

Martin Mansergh was born in 1946 in Woking, the son of Nicholas Mansergh, the Tipperary-born distinguished Irish and Commonwealth historian. He studied at Oxford where he became an authority on eighteenth century French history. He is Special Adviser to the Taoiseach on Northern Ireland, Economic and Social Matters. He is married to a Scotswoman with five children and runs the family farm in Tipperary with his brother.

For many of us, what the Border means has evolved a good deal over our lifetime. My father, a historian, worked in England, but regularly went home to Tipperary, where he owned a farm, to write and be with relatives. In the 1950s, as children, we spent our summers in Tipperary, but the rest of the year we were cared for by Eleanor McClenaghan from Islandmagee. I was very fond of her, but growing up when Pope John XXIII was much admired across the religious divide, I remonstrated good-humouredly at some mild anti-popery. From Tipperary, the Border seemed distant. Few neighbours visited Northern Ireland. The unionist government was unattractive, but seemed destined to continue in perpetuity. Northern Ireland was better off than the South, and had no particular incentive to rejoin it. An early history lesson was how Ulster unionists effectively abandoned their co-religionists in Donegal, Cavan and Monaghan, while Southern unionists preferred to keep even a self-governing Ireland united. Locally, the War of Independence was a vivid memory, and what had been achieved since, despite setbacks and disappointments, a source of pride. But unity, a national aim, was privately regarded as improbable. Southern Protestants, then a somewhat more numerous small community, had to respect the over-whelming Catholic majority and their democratic right to order things as they saw fit, but valued the toleration of their own relative freedom and prosperity, while seeking to be good neighbours and, where applicable, employers.

In the mid-1960s, the Rev. Ian Paisley came to the Oxford Union, when I was a student, to deliver a crude assault on Catholicism, playing shamelessly to prejudices not too far below the surface of English life. Ireland under Lemass was on the move, and even Northern Ireland un-der Terence O'Neill seemed to be opening up to the winds of change. The scale of grievance and the limitations of mere expressions of goodwill were not at first fully under-stood. For anyone susceptible at all to the student radi-calism of the 1960s, there was no contest in deciding what side one was on in relation to the Civil Rights campaign, which brought the border much closer to home.

In 1969, my father was under no illusion that the IRA would be back. A gaping hole, which suddenly opened in one of our fields in about 1970, was symbolic in more ways than one. Few Southern Protestants wished to be tarred with unionist excesses, and the advent of the Trou-bles probably completed their process of identification with the Irish state, away from the Border where they caused some to shrink back.

Everyone in Ireland lived, through television and other news, in close proximity to the traumatic events in North-ern Ireland. Most people in the South looked forward to seeing the Border go, but peacefully and by agreement. While identifying strongly with the injuries and grievances of nationalists, they did not accept dreadful deeds committed in their name. Having at first underestimated unionist resilience, because of its deep fractures, they slowly came to terms with the persistence of another tradition. The Troubles gave impetus to the development of pluralism in the South, arguably an easier part of the problem.

For many reasons, people began to venture more across the Border. Northern politicians were invited South to put their case. Common EU membership since 1973 progressively reduced the economic significance of the Border and many physical marks, such as customs and security barriers (and even the absurd name-sign, "Ye Olde Border Inn") have now disappeared. Political relations with Britain greatly improved, with both Governments working in partnership in recent years. While Northern Ireland is much like the rest of Ireland, its appearance is also marked by its continuing UK membership.

Even if less visible, the Border still retains significance. Peace, stability and reconciliation are necessary goals in their own right, irrespective of future developments. The price of peace for the South is continuing constructive engagement with both communities in the North. Since the 1960s, increased North/South co-operation has become an indispensable part of any solution.

More of us have come to recognise the virtues and strengths of people in the North as well as the tragedy of lives cut short. If we are sometimes impatient at the slow improvement in relations following the end of conflict, we have to maintain the effort, through thick and thin, because so much is at stake for all of us. In regard to peace, at least, Ireland is indivisible.

Gary Mitchell

Gary Mitchell was born in 1965 in Rathcoole, the largest working class Protestant housing estate in Northern Ireland. His first play, The World, the Flesh and the Devil, *was adapted for radio and won the BBC's Young Playwrights competition in 1991. Gary wrote a further ten radio plays between 1993 and 1997. His work for the theatre includes* Independent Voice, That Driving Ambition, In a Little World of Our Own, Sinking, As the Beast Sleeps, Tearing the Loom, *and* Trust. *He has also written for television and cinema.*

When I was a boy in school studying geography, part of our lesson was devoted to drawing maps and on one particular day we had to trace the British Isles from an atlas. After a lot of practice and with great pride I could complete the task without the atlas. The Border between Northern Ireland and the Republic of Ireland was the most notable feature of my drawings. It seemed that the importance of Northern Ireland as a separate entity on one island and an integral part of another was more important in the playground than in any test because I don't remember getting extra marks for my superb sketches.

In Sunday school I was taught that Catholics were the Antichrist and outside of school I was informed that the Republic of Ireland was a Catholic country that was trying to take over my Protestant country and make us all become Catholics. Not that I knew what the difference was, but I drew the Border thicker each time just to be on the safe side.

Through my childhood and teenage years, my desire to man that Border grew in exact proportion to my fear of the Catholic community. The community that was continually invading my country from the Republic, taking my people's jobs, houses, land and women and unlikely to stop there. If I ever met a group of Catholic invaders from over the Border, where they belong, they would try to shoot me, bomb me or eat my children. The fear grew and would only diminish in the shadow of the Border and so, to me, we couldn't build it high enough or wide enough.

When I became a young man I demanded my place in society as a warrior who would rid this beautiful country of its enemies, and I met the Catholics. We fought at first, violence failed. We argued secondly, shouting failed. Now, we talk. We debate. We discuss. The fear is gone now, replaced with regret and sorrow. I recognise our differences and I see clearly what we have in common.

I think now that the Republic of Ireland wants to invade Northern Ireland about as much as Great Britain wants to keep it within the United Kingdom.

My work as a playwright has taken me all over the United Kingdom, into the Republic of Ireland and further afield. I believe I've discovered a great deal about how the outside world looks in at us, if it can be bothered at all. "The war is over," they say. I think it is only beginning. The real solution and the reality of an everlasting peace is that it will only come from the people who live in Northern Ireland. Interference from England, the Republic of Ireland and the US, whilst being perhaps a necessary evil, has at times been helpful, but is more often a hindrance.

It is my opinion, in order to understand the complexity of Northern Ireland, you must live here.

I still draw the Border thickly in the tiny maps in my head, but now it is to remind me that the people of Northern Ireland are mainly responsible for the "Troubles". And it is they who have the ability, though perhaps not the desire, to move away from them and leave them behind forever.

Paddy Monaghan

Paddy Monaghan works as a Reconciliation Facilitator funded under the Programme for Peace and Reconciliation, is Secretary of the Evangelical Catholic Initiative in the Republic of Ireland and co-editor of Adventures in Reconciliation *(1998) — testimonies of Christians who are building bridges of friendship, North and South.*

When I think of the Border, I think not just of the division between the six counties and the twenty-six, but of the even bigger emotional border in people's hearts and minds and the incredible pain it has given rise to. But things are changing!

I grew up in Kells, County Meath and often heard people speak about the "black Protestants in the North"! In school history classes, the emphasis was on how England had oppressed the Irish over the centuries and how the Border was forced upon us, causing great anger and a sense of injustice and alienation, particularly in Northern nationalists.

In 1969, when the "Troubles" broke out, I empathised with the nationalists in the North, particularly as they embraced the Civil Rights agenda of one-man-one-vote and an end to discrimination in housing and jobs. I was really saddened when, in some areas, the Catholic community turned from a protest of non-violent civil disobedience to accepting the IRA as their defenders. At that stage, the Border for me was a line of defence, keeping me safe from the injustice, discrimination, intolerance and violence "up there".

After Bloody Sunday in 1972, I experienced real anger against the British. I took part in a student march to the British Embassy, where the anger took deeper hold as we chanted: "One dead! Two dead! . . . Thirteen dead!"

A year later, I came into a personal faith in Jesus Christ and experienced real repentance for my hatred and had a desire to build bridges of friendship with Protestant Christians, and between North and South, Ireland and England. Among the 250,000 Protestants within Northern Ireland who would identify themselves as evangelical, some 100,000 would not accept that it is possible to be a practising Roman Catholic and a committed Christian. For many of these, "Home Rule is Rome Rule", and "South of the Border" is a no-go area. Encountering these evangelical Christians brings, initially, the inevitable painful realisation that they do not accept me as a Christian. I have, however, found that the mutual sharing of our personal faith in Christ establishes a basis upon which we can talk, without rancour, about the major difficulties they have with the Catholic Church.

I attended a number of conferences in Belfast and began to build friendships with individual Protestant Christians, one of whom was an RUC man. I began to see that any place is as good or as bad as the friendships you have with people who live there.

As the IRA campaign gathered momentum and more policemen were murdered, I felt it was important to express repentance, not just in words but also in action — so over the years I have attended the funerals of many policemen. It was really appreciated that I, as a Southern Catholic Christian, would come to "mourn with those who mourn". After the IRA murder of four RUC men at the Border, I drove to Newry RUC station with a bouquet of flowers. It deeply touched the murdered men's colleagues that a Southern Catholic would come with a token of the genuine sympathy of fellow Catholics from Dublin. Every time I pass the Border, I pray that God will heal the divisions represented by it.

After the Omagh bomb, I attended the funeral of one of the victims, Esther Gibson, a Free Presbyterian Sunday school teacher in Fivemiletown. The family really appreciated my being there and I was invited for sandwiches to the Orange Hall afterwards, where I talked with Rev. William McCrea.

On 3 July 1999 I participated with 120 others (including some 40 Catholic Christians) in a Day of Prayer and Fasting at Drumcree, asking God to defuse the anger and bring a peaceful resolution to a very tense situation. Thank God, He answered our prayer and that of many others. During the day, I went down to the barricade and spoke to some very angry Orangemen. For one man, the root of his anger lay in an encounter, as a youth, with a fellow Roman Catholic workmate, who said that if his priest asked him to murder him, he would. I asked his forgiveness for these evil words, even spoken in malicious jest, from someone from within my community. The effect was almost immediate. His anger dissipated and when I asked if I could pray for God's blessing on him, he agreed, then deciding to return home to tend his farm.

This encounter is a microcosm of what the Border has come to mean — a symbol of the deep hurt that people from both communities have experienced. It also showed me how important it is that we listen to each other and take ownership for the wrongs that have come from within our respective communities, even to expressing repentance and asking for forgiveness. I think that, whatever about the political Border, this is the only way to deal with the emotional border which has led to such hatred, bitterness and pain.

As a Christian, I see Christ as my role model in building cross-border friendships. Jesus confronted "borders" at every level of Jewish society and beyond. He challenges His followers likewise to cross all barriers and in the process build friendships without fences and a Church without borders, open to all people who love and serve him.

Ireland has become known as a place where Christians murder each other and has brought great dishonour to the Name of Christ. It is encouraging to see that many Christians are starting to find one another across barriers that have been not just of doctrine alone but of culture, language and history. Can we not, North and South, see the Border as a challenge to be deliberately travelled across again and again in both directions, thus eroding the emotional dimension of the Border and building meaningful relationships which reflect the mind of Christ? So Ireland may again become, by God's grace, a "light to the nations".

Ellen Mongan

Ellen Mongan is a pre-school teacher and was the first member of her family to go on to third-level education. She became the first Traveller to be elected to a public body, namely Tuam Town Commissioners, in 1994. Ellen is involved in many cross-community development projects. She hopes, someday, to meet Nelson Mandela, a person she believes to be of one of the greatest to grace this earth.

I was born into a roadside encampment in the west of Ireland in 1964, at a time when the Civil Rights marches were at their height in the United States and soon to emerge onto the streets closer to home. I began my life very much a nomad, knowing no boundaries of time, class or geography. I come from a people who historically have never laid claim to land, belonging only to the "long acre": the roadside. My earliest memory of the North of Ireland is of my mother engrossed in an old "Pam" transistor radio in our trailer, listening to the evening news. I was around eight years of age; this was a regular evening ritual. My sister and I knew this was a time not to disturb my mother, we were barred from this event.

It was never in the psyche of a Traveller to be duly concerned with the affairs of the settled community, so little discussion was given to the "Northern Troubles"; with hindsight, my community in many ways were no different to the settled people when it came to the North. One stark difference is the Travellers' movement during the Troubles, freely crossing over this Border. The Border was non-existent to us, our thinking being if nothing physically existed, then what was all the fuss about.

I remember in my early teens thinking, actually believing, that Belfast was a thousand miles away. I was of the belief that once you passed over the Border, you were entering the "Wild West"; that's if you survived the Border crossing! These myths were fed to me through TV news in particular. Normality didn't exist up North; well, no news item ever portrayed the daily experience of having to live.

I suppose these assumptions/stereotypes were part of the reason that I did not travel in the North, until I was in my mid-twenties. My first time in Belfast was not by choice. I had to hastily return from Scotland; unable to get a flight, I had to travel by ferry from Stranraer to Larne. On arrival, I was greeted by an armoured tank and British soldiers. They were hanging out the sides with their guns at the ready. Due to my fear and anxiety, I failed, like TV news people, to see ordinary people going about their daily lives. My only concern was to get across the Border fast. Amazing, now the Border mattered.

My level of awareness increased with my personal development. I could see many similarities in the struggle for emancipation. I now take great joy in travelling North with my friends and family. On their first journey, I am reminded of myself in their facial expression as they cross the Border for the first time.

Christy Moore

Christy Moore was born in Newbridge, County Kildare to Andy Moore and Nancy Power on 7 May 1945. He has been singing since he could talk and recording since 1969. He lives in Dublin with Valerie and their family Andy, Juno and Padraic. He loves to sing.

Dear Paddy

Thank you for your letter and enclosures. I've tried and tried to write the little bit you asked me to write and I've not managed to get anywhere. Pointless, stupid, trite lines keep coming off my nib, my wastepaper basket is full of shite about the Border. The only thing I can think to say is "Fuck the Border". But you probably need more than three words.

Sincerely

Christy Moore

Sing along:

> "Border, Border, Border, Border, Border
> This Border, that Border, the other Border
> Border, Border, Border, Border
> Fuck the Border."

Austen Morgan

Austen Morgan was born and grew up in Derry. He attended university in Bristol and Belfast. In his first career as an academic writer, he published books on twentieth-century Irish and British history. He is now a barrister in London. He will be publishing a legal textbook on the Belfast Agreement in December 1999.

How I Learned to Love the Border

I have had occasion to dwell on the meaning of partition at three points in my life: growing up in Derry in the 1950s and 1960s; during the futile IRA campaign of the last 30 years; and as a lawyer studying the 1998 Belfast Agreement.

The Irish Border as a Real Divide

Being born several miles from an international frontier makes one extraordinarily conscious of difference, not least because of the minority/majority problem in Northern Ireland.

I recall crossing the Border regularly, in one family car after another, with much stamping of paper. Derry Catholics, and especially Protestants, were alert to their level of social provision compared with County Donegal; northwest Ulster survived (in the minds of older people) as the hinterland of the city, though many in the Republic envied the benefits available in Northern Ireland.

These were courtesy of the United Kingdom, Attlee's post-war Labour government pioneering the welfare state. I and my siblings were the first generation to benefit from the National Health Service. We were also guaranteed free education, though Stormont caved in to Catholic sectarianism. If we had been born several miles on the other side of the Border, I suspect none of us would have had the opportunities we have enjoyed.

The Irish government (Eamon de Valera was Taoiseach until 1959, and President until 1973) meant virtually nothing. Blather about a united Ireland was combined with no help to Northern Catholics (other than with the pretend national language), and the continuing failure to develop good neighbourly relations with the provincial government in Belfast.

I remember a primary school class mate in the 1956–62 IRA campaign, describing an Irish tricolour he spotted as a "Catholic Badge".

Dying — and Killing — for Ireland
I was involved in the Civil Rights movement (though have achieved some critical distance with maturity). Socialism was then my cause rather than nationalism. I welcomed Sunningdale as an extraordinary British concession; and regretted its failure (partly due to SDLP political greed).

Caitlín Ní Houliháin never attracted me; I preferred more human, complex women. I found the republican version of Irish history — encountered researching a doctorate at Queen's in the 1970s — to be intellectually bankrupt.

As for the strategy and tactics of the IRA, we have the recent cost of the Troubles survey: 3,585 people were killed up to 3 December 1997; 87 per cent by paramilitaries (59 per cent by republicans and 28 per cent by loyalists); only 11 per cent by the security forces (yet too many

Irish intellectuals have contributed to ignorant cosmopolitan views of British imperialism).

Ireland is extremely politically backward on the question of partition. Nationalists cannot forget 1920 (and they
have yet to understand why constitutional division occurred). The Indian subcontinent has dealt with the
problem more maturely. And Cyprus has shown an ability
at times to embrace federalism.

The best comparator of constitutional and revolution-
ary republicanism is Hindu nationalism, with the sectarian BJP the closest contemporary analogue to Sinn Féin.

"Ireland's right to determine her own destiny," the new
Catholic Mayor of Derry had proclaimed in 1920, "[would]
come about whether the Protestants of Ulster like[d] it or
not." They didn't. And it didn't. And it most probably
won't.

The Belfast Agreement
This (to give it its proper name) has been characterised by
Seamus Mallon as "Sunningdale for slow learners".

The slow learners are obviously the republicans (as-
suming they are embracing constitutional politics). They
are not the Ulster Unionists; David Trimble first embraced voluntary power-sharing in 1975. And John Hume
boycotted the 1982 assembly, when a stand should have
been taken for democracy against terrorism.

The Belfast Agreement constitutionally is a partitionist
settlement. It provides for the ending of the Irish constitutional claim. A few rhetorical concessions were made by
the United Kingdom government (exaggerated by "no"
unionists and republicans alike).

A united Ireland will only come about if the people of Northern Ireland so consent, and the people of the Republic then vote to take them in.

Institutionally, the Belfast Agreement is less than Sunningdale. And we waited 25 years for it.

Strand One is similar, though based this time on sectarian rather than centrist principles. If getting Sinn Féin into the four-party involuntary coalition is proving difficult, wait until the DUP starts being in but not of the regional administration.

Strand Two is a great deal less than it would have been in 1974 with the Council of Ireland. And the idea of practical co-operation across an international frontier is now acceptable to some nationalists and more unionists.

Strand Three — the Council of the Isles — is completely new, and balances united Ireland fantasies with the reality of a these-islands-approach — long known to the real people of Ireland in communion with their Scottish, English and Welsh neighbours.

Though I have written a textbook for lawyers, *The Belfast Agreement: A Practical Legal Analysis*, neither I nor the democratic leaders in the two states can do much more. "Waiting for Provo" is still the only show in town.

Jane Morrice

Jane Morrice was elected to the Northern Ireland Assembly as the Women's Coalition member for North Down. She is the former head of the European Commission Office in Northern Ireland. By profession she is a journalist.

As a teenager living in Belfast in the years before the "Troubles", a day spent "going down to Dublin" was an exciting adventure. Whether we travelled by train or hitchhiked to save the fare, crossing the Border was a non-event. Those were the 1960s, when young people had nothing to fear but being found out.

Dublin even then was a cosmopolitan city. I remember marvelling at the flocks of young Spanish and French students who gathered at the bowling alley in Stillorgan or the discos in downtown Dublin. For some reason, they never came to Belfast.

As a child, I often travelled with the family to the Republic during the Easter or summer break. My father always made a point of remarking on the poor quality of the roads South of the Border. If we closed our eyes, he said, we could feel the difference between North and South through the suspension of the car.

In those days, crossing the Border was all about going on holiday. The culture was different. The atmosphere was relaxed. The roads may have been bad, but the "craic" was great. We had nothing to dread but the thought of going back to school.

With the 1970s came the "Troubles", when growing up in Northern Ireland became synonymous with getting out.

Every step I took towards finding a career was done with the aim of crossing a border for good. Eventually I did. First to France, then to the US and then to Brussels in 1980, where I lived for seven years.

Living in continental Europe had a tremendous impact on my life. It developed the seeds of my understanding that a border exists only to be crossed. I appreciated that there was difference on either side, but that difference was to be cherished, not derided. By travelling, meeting new people and discovering new cultures, I could broaden my horizons and learn more about humanity.

Working as a journalist specialising in Third World development, I got the chance to cross many borders. In Africa and Asia, I saw at first hand the real needs of people fighting for survival. In refugee camps along the Thai/Cambodian border, I saw men, women and children used as human barriers to protect the border against attack. I wondered then, as I do now, what line on a map could be held in higher esteem than the life of a child?

When I returned to Belfast in 1987, I was saddened to see that little had changed. People were suffering the same pain in the so-called "civilised" world as their neighbours in the developing world. It became clear that the Border dividing the North and South was not a single line on the map. The same "Border" separated schools, housing estates, towns, cities and even families within Northern Ireland. When the Berlin Wall was broken down by "people power" in 1989, new walls were being erected by "people fear" in Belfast.

My involvement in politics was and remains an attempt on my part to break down the psychological barriers that prevent neighbours from crossing the street to shake each other's hand in mutual respect. In the Northern Ireland Women's Coalition, we managed to prove that it is possible. As a group of women with nothing in common but our determination to create a better life for all, we cross the divide in every direction. We do not attempt to change each other's views, but we do try to stand in each other's shoes.

My travels abroad helped confirm my desire to challenge the accepted norm in Northern Ireland — that the Border is there to be broken down or built up. There is, I believe, another way round. If we can break down the psychological barriers that treat people who are different as "alien" and learn instead to respect that difference, then the concept of "the Border" becomes less relevant.

The last thing I want to do when I cross a border anywhere in the world is open my eyes and see no difference. Diversity should be valued. The only similarity that should exist across borders is the right for all to live in dignity.

Paul Muldoon

Paul Muldoon, who was born in County Armagh in 1951, is the author of eight collections of poetry, most recently Hay *and* The Annals of Chile, *which won the T.S. Eliot Prize in 1994. His* New Selected Poems 1968–94 *won the 1997 Irish Times Prize for Poetry. Paul Muldoon is Howard G.B. Clark '21 Professor in the Humanities at Princeton University and Professor of Poetry at the University of Oxford.*

na gCaorach." "*Scairbh na gCaorach,*" I chewed on my
    foul madams,
"is now better known as 'Emyvale'
though the Irish name means 'the sheep-steeps' or the
    'rampart of rams'."

"'Rampart of rams?' That makes sense. It was the image of
    an outcrop of shale
with a particularly sheer
drop that my ancestors, the 'people of the veil',

held before them as they drove their flocks from tier to
    tier
through Algeria, Mali and Libya all the way up to Armagh,
    Monaghan and Louth
with — you'll like this — a total disregard for any frontier."

III

"Patrick Regan?" A black-coated RUC man was
    unwrapping a scarf from his mouth
and flicking back and forth from my uncle's licence to his
    face.
"Have you any news of young Sean South?

The last I heard he was suffering from a bad case
of lead poisoning. Maybe he's changed his name to Gone
    West?"
I knew rightly he could trace

us by way of that bottle of Redbreast
under my seat, that carton of Players, that bullion-chest of
  butter.
I knew rightly we'd fail each and every test

they might be preparing behind the heavy, iron shutters
even now being raised aloft
by men carrying belt-saws and blow-torches and
  bolt-cutters.

IV

As he turned to me again, thirty years later in Rotterdam,
  the Tuareg doffed
his sky-blue scarf. "Back in those days I saw no risk
in sleeping under hedges. As a matter of fact I preferred a
  thorn hedge to a hayloft

because — you'll like this — it reminded me of the
  tamarisks
along the salt route into Timbuktu."
He crossed his forearms lightly under his armpits as if he
  might be about to frisk

himself, then smiled as he handed me the sky-blue
winding-cloth and a clunking water gourd.
"It had been my understanding that *Scairbh na gCaorach*
  meant 'the crossing of ewes'

for *scairbh* means not 'a ledge' but 'a ford' or, more
    specifically, 'a shallow ford'."
And he immediately set off at a jog-trot down an
    unapproved road
Near Aughnacloy or Swanlinbar or Lifford.

V

"It had always been my sense," I hear him still, "that the
    gad fades into the goad
and the spur fades into the flank
and the fastness fades into no fixed abode

and the Black Pig's Dyke fades into the piggybank
and Ham fades into Japheth
and the point fades into the point-blank

and the polymaths fade into the meths
where the ends somehow begin to fade into the means
and the sheugh fades into the shibboleth

and the timbre fades into the tambourine
and the quiddity fades into the *quid pro quo*
and — you'll like this, I know — the bourne fades into the
    boreen."

Dervla Murphy

Dervla Murphy is an internationally renowned travel writer, whose books include Eight Feet in the Andes, In Ethiopia with a Mule, South from the Limpopo *and* A Place Apart — *the last about Northern Ireland.*

Ten years after the Border's creation I was created — born into a family vigorously republican on the paternal side. By 1940 my fanatical genes had taken over and to me the Border seemed a vile injustice inflicted on an innocent little nation by a malignant next-door bully. It explained why Ireland was, ostensibly, neutral in a war which I hoped Hitler would win. Evidently I was slow on the up-take; I never noticed those tens of thousands of my com-patriots who were emigrating to fight in our enemy's army and work in our enemy's munitions factories.

By 1945, the Border was arousing in me the sort of crazy teenage emotionalism later associated with pop star worship. I attended many open-air anti-partition rallies, wrote long passionate "poems" on the subject and ex-plained to a network of pen pals on other continents that the Border represented Britain's refusal, for devious im-perialist reasons, to grant freedom to all of Ireland. Also, I day-dreamed about joining the New IRA and performing feats of heroism which would somehow reunite my coun-try. Blowing up Stromont in the middle of the night was a particularly satisfying daydream. I can't remember whether I chose the middle of the night to save my own skin or to avoid collateral damage.

At that time my rage was primitive, territorial; I wanted our flag to be flying over the six counties. I don't

recall feeling any anger about discrimination against nationalists. The conflict, as I in my ignorance perceived it,
was simply British versus Irish — the unionists being
merely a minority of pro-British settlers for whom there
was surely enough room in the United Kingdom to which
they professed such fervent loyalty. In my most fevered
anti-partitionist phase I never thought in Catholic versus
Protestant terms. Despite my psyche having been dyed
green in childhood, I grew up free of any taint of religious
bigotry, perhaps because both my parents came of healthy
mongrel stock: Irish Catholic, French Huguenot, Scots
Presbyterian, Italian Jewish.

By the age of 17, my reading of history had extended
beyond Dorothy MacArdle, Dan Breen et al. and I gradually came to realise that in times past the British ruling
class had treated their own peasantry, industrial workers
and non-conformist Christians no more kindly than they
treated Irish Catholics. Was it not absurd, in 1950, to view
Britain as "the enemy"? Like it or not, our 700-year-old
relationship was "special", often — though not always —
destructive for Ireland but anyway a fact of life in the
twentieth century. I remained staunchly anti-partitionist
but with a slight shift of perspective; the unionists were
coming into focus as the main defenders of the Border,
though as yet I had no understanding of their profound
insecurity, of their parlous position as an inconvenient (to
Britain) residue of the failed attempt to absorb Ireland
into the UK as Wales and Scotland had been absorbed.

In 1963, I began to travel outside Europe and, having
lived for longish periods in remote and sometimes troubled regions, the Border fell into place as a comparatively
trivial problem, harrowing for the victims of violence and

discrimination, but minor in global terms. By 1969, the Border looked to me like an artificial frontier drawn on the map in a clumsy effort to solve a psycho-political problem. A problem rooted in centuries of greed, prejudice, injustice, suspicion, fear and hatred. Hatred? A strong, nasty word. A confusing, limiting, destructive emotion. But everywhere it is the chemical reaction when those other ingredients are combined in history's test-tube.

Significantly, I myself never set foot across the Border until 1976 — when I at once fell in love with the Northern Irish, en masse. That journey was prompted by my shame of suddenly realising that I knew nothing about the complexities of daily life in Northern Ireland and was totally dependent on unreliable media interpretations of events. Other journeys followed and eventually I wrote a book about my own reactions to the problem.

By 1984, when the Forum Report was published, the Border seemed acceptable to me. A united Ireland, though still emotionally desirable and practically sensible, had vanished over the mental horizon of all but the most unrealistic of my compatriots. Ireland's two regions had grown apart — literally. Each had matured (or failed to mature) as a separate entity. In Northern Ireland many of the prosperous greens had become more "British" than they themselves perhaps recognised. And many of the deprived greens were bitterly antagonistic to the "Free State" — this anachronism a symptom of their estrangement from the "Staters" who abandoned them to unionist domination.

In the Republic, the majority had developed an allergy to thinking or feeling about Northern Ireland. Only a rump remained interested, a responsible rump of politicians and would-be peace-makers and a lawless rump of paramilitary supporters. Whenever I returned from a visit to the North, eager to engage my neighbours in a discussion about the problem, eyes glazed over, shoulders shrugged, hands were waved limply, dismissing the subject. "Why get involved with the shower up there? Aren't they six of one and half a dozen of another? Let them sort themselves out and leave us in peace!" The Republic has its own identity and no longer thought of itself as maimed by the amputation of the six counties. The Border had become a permanent fixture — vaguely regrettable, especially among the older generation, but no longer a source of communal grief and rage as it was during my youth.

In September 1993, I returned from a five-month cycle tour of South Africa and within 48 hours of leaving Johannesburg found myself in Belfast, promoting a new book. I was shaken, then, by my changed attitude to the problem. All the concerned sympathy I had felt for everyone in Northern Ireland, since 1976, seemed to drain away. Spontaneously diagnosed a mass-neurosis, a silly quarrel kept going by people who didn't know how lucky they were to be able to indulge in all this British government-subsidised nonsense. Compared to the vast majority of South Africans, even the least fortunate Northern Irish are pampered. The Border then looked like a tragic fence enclosing people in an unnatural reservation which allowed orange quasi-religious bigotry and green cultural prejudice to flourish in isolation from the real world. I fantasised about airlifting the lot to South Africa (unsubsidised) for a year-long exposure to 40 per cent unemployment without a dole, gross over-crowding in tiny dwellings, under-staffed and under-equipped schools and hospitals, a surfeit of guns held by desperate criminals, an ever-increasing murder rate and a police force who regularly shoot robbers dead, no questions asked.

Quite soon, I recovered from that extreme over-reaction — but only partially. At intervals since then — particularly when the mass-neurosis surfaces at Drumcree — my post-South Africa exasperation is reactivated.

Under direct rule from Westminster, the unionists' power to discriminate against nationalists was greatly reduced. But that regime lowered Northern Ireland to the level of a turbulent colony dependent on Pax Brittanica, with the rulers' security forces in practice favouring one of the warring tribes, as so often happened in Africa and Asia when the Empire was at its zenith. Moreover, the Northern Irish had become a discarded people; the Republic didn't want them, Britain didn't want them. But everyone wanted peace within the Border, hence the Good Friday Agreement. A decade ago, who would have believed that such a compromise was possible? In May 1998, I rejoiced when the Border was formally accepted, both by the citizens of the Republic (cheerfully) and by Northern Ireland's greens (resignedly).

For many years past, I have opposed militarism in all its manifestations from NATO to the IRA — which is not quite the same thing as being a committed Quaker-style pacifist. I acknowledge that certain conflicts are not amenable to non-violent resolutions and in April 1998 I had reluctantly to face the fact that without IRA violence the Good Friday Agreement would never have happened. It is unfashionable to face this fact, but hypocritical to deny it. Neither side won Northern Ireland's heart-breaking 30 years' war, but it did lead to a fundamental change in the significance of the Border.

Nuala O'Faolain

Nuala O'Faolain is a writer and a columnist with The Irish Times. *She has been a university lecturer and a BBC and RTE television producer. Her autobiography,* Are You Somebody, *was published in 1996.*

(The following was originally published in and is reproduced with the kind permission of The Irish Times*)*

The turn in Ireland's fortunes is summed up for me by the Border itself. I mean the actual, physical Border where it is at its most formal, on the main road from Belfast to Dublin.

I remember my father furtively turning away his face, while the car waited at the Border there, because he didn't want anyone to see the distress it caused him to cross on to British territory.

And wait is what cars used to do, because there was a piece of paper called a triptych that drivers had to have and there were slow bureaucratic manoeuvres to do with customs and excise. This was even before the Troubles.

When they came, the customs situation was simplified because the customs hut was blown up or burnt down. But the road crossing became increasingly difficult, what with military and paramilitary exactions.

You never knew how long you might have to wait in a queue before bumping over the ramp and through the Army post where your number was scrutinised, at best, and where you might well be detained for hours, at worst. Well, that wasn't the worst.

People were killed or were wounded on that stretch of road between Ravensdale forest on the Dundalk side and Newry in the North. It was one of the most stained places.

You should see it now. No-man's-land used to be the epitome of the difficult, unlovely landscape of Ireland. It was a stretch of small, marshy fields, haphazardly marked out by gorse and briars and meandering ditches.

History had left crumbling two-room cottages dotted all over it, hardly seeming to belong to the same era as the dun steel of the British Army surveillance posts up on the lumpy hills. Now, that old land, that somebody must once have hopelessly tried to farm, is being in-filled at speed. New ramps lead to a fuel farm where the huge lorries that keep this First World island in luxuries gather to exchange behemoth signals.

The hotel at the Border gets bigger and bigger. There's a health and leisure centre there. The petrol stations incorporate shops, coffee bars, information centres, telephones. It is true that the road itself is still narrow, but work has begun on widening and straightening it. The furze bushes topple before the JCBs.

And new houses with PVC gables and patio extensions and dormer windows are rising over the ruins of the old cottages. This Border is on the move into suburbia. Soon it will be one giant motorway service station.

The British Army is still there, but not so that a passing motorist would notice. The memory of its looming presence has faded. There used to be a big corrugated-iron encampment through which the traffic going north and south was funnelled. Then the encampment went, but the road was still diverted through its ghost. Now they've straightened out the road.

Up on the bank there are two little stone memorials, with flowers in front of them, to British soldiers who died here. Above those again there's a watching-post. But soon you will be passing by too quickly to notice. In the tense hours leading up to polling day for the referendums in July 1998, soldiers had set up roadblocks along the routes to Belfast and were checking licences. But that's abnormal now. All this will soon be a highway.

Cars will whiz from Dublin to Belfast, and the sight and the feel and the memories awoken by particular places like Balbriggan and Drogheda and Dundalk will be forgotten. The variations in the texture of Ireland will disappear. Belfast to Dublin will be like Antwerp to Lille or Stuttgart to Nancy. You'll speed along on top of the history. Lidice, Hoesca, Poyntzpass. They'll all equally be names on signposts.

This is what is going to happen. No matter how long it takes. The money-changers on the Border will abandon the old farmhouses and cottages they so incongruously use as their offices, and redbrick villas with conservatories will rise on their sites. In five years' time — if Britain enters EMU — there will just be euros, North and South. It will be more and more difficult for the smugglers along the half-forgotten Border to make a living, much less enough to supply their families with the statutory 20-room haciendas with gold-plated bathrooms.

In any case, their sons and daughters will all be study-ing fine art in Florence or aerospace design in Dresden on Euroschemes. They will not be interested in the ancestral skills of filling in the tag-holes in cows' ears with paste, or injecting badly made growth hormones into young pigs.

Maybe there'll be casino ships or floating liquor su-permarkets moored in Carlingford Lough, staffed by Kurds and Moldovans. But probably there'll be nothing to tell that two sovereign jurisdictions abut along this line. It will be like going from Holland into Belgium. There is nothing to mark a Border there. It takes a while to know you have left a country with such-and-such a name and arrived at a place with a different one. Eventually, of course, the cultural differences show up. In Ireland, there will be much better bread and cakes in the bakeries in the north of the country, and the breads will have different names than in the southern part. Humour will be blacker in the north. Cars will be more washed. The south will be more sociable and much more ready to have fun. Little things.

Before, when I was growing up, Ireland was at peace, but it was the peace, North and South, of perfectly achieved repression. This new peace — the coming of which is now inevitable, let who will stand in its way — will be more life-giving. There will be space to move in, because the big contentions that filled all the space be-tween us will dissolve with each passing year back into the blur called the past.

The walking wounded from the Troubles will move among us. They won't even have each other to talk to: there are going to be different rates of recovery from the last 30 years in different parts of the island. On the loyalist estates in Portadown or in the alienated villages of South Armagh, or in East Fermanagh where one community felt itself the object of a planned campaign of extinction, the inner life of the people will be very slow to change.

Change it will, however. The alder and willow scrub in the low fields in the pass between Dundalk and Newry will be covered over with the sheds and loading-bays of an entrepot.

Where now Spanish broom has escaped from old gardens, satellite dishes will be planted in concrete yards behind security railings. The emotion that filled my father and so many others will wither in the neon glare. Whatever the passions of the new Ireland will be, they won't be the ones that once rose from the land itself. "What Border?" visitors will say, glancing out from their speeding cars at nothing much.

© *Irish Times Ltd.*

Ardal O'Hanlon

Ardal O'Hanlon is a writer and comedian and is probably best known for his role as Father Dougal in the Channel Four sitcom Father Ted. *He is currently working on his second novel and involved in the rearing of some small children.*

To the people of my home town, Carrickmacross, the Border didn't exist at all. It was but an arbitrary and imaginary line on a map, a fairytale trail of breadcrumbs, a psychological barrier at best that divided a nation and a people. In some quarters, you couldn't even use the actual word "Border" if you knew what was good for you. It was spat out like a particularly sour damson.

But of course, no matter how much you ignored it politically and willed it away emotionally, the Border was there. In fact, it had become over time a real and physical proposition, a geographical feature as permanent as any ridge or river, a faultline of hucksters' gaudy mansions linked together by a higgledy-piggledy wall of lookout towers and fortifications and filling stations and arms dumps and drumlins and car graveyards and checkpoints and bombed-out customs posts and attitudes as hard as tungsten. It had become a welt on the back of a galley slave.

To either side of this eyesore, there lay a no-man's-land, a buffer zone of ragwort and rumour, both deadly in their respective ways. This murmuring poisonous swathe gave refuge to all sorts of desperadoes — smugglers and gunmen and Country 'n' Irish superstars. Flushing out the latter was a relatively easy task, it was like looking for hay in a haystack in the Land of Hay. A species of big-haired, big-hatted, big-hearted balladeers, they sang loudly and often of the pain of living in places like Castleblayney, tunes as tired as turfcutters at sundown. Theirs were the names that stilled our childish play and indeed the flow of our very blood — Philomena Begley, Susan McCann, Anna McGoldrick, Gloria, to mention but a few. In any other area of any other country in the world they would have been simply known as housewives.

I suppose it would be harsh to blame them or the likes of Big Tom of driving men insane and thereby perpetuating the Troubles. If anything, their music, for want of a better word for that dreary derivative sentimental mind-numbing soul-deadening monotonous sound that leaked from their lungs like liquid Mogadon, should have acted as a balm, a soporific to men of violence. I do blame them, however, here and now for soundtracking every social gathering and subsequent sexual failure, for forcing desire to wear a sensible woolly jumper and a bobble hat. It is entirely their fault that I ended up more often than not puking in a puddle of regret than jiving at the come-hither toes of a sultry Northern lass.

But it wasn't all fun living along the Border, for its shadow extended over every part of your daily grind. After the Monaghan bombing, you feared for your own safety and that of your town. You became even more nosy and suspicious than before, if that was genetically possible. You heard first-hand accounts of the war from your relatives in Armagh. An old uncle of mine with a wasting disease couldn't remember anything except verbatim news bulletins about the killings. You took seriously the bomb warning phoned to your house after midnight, even if it was only a disgruntled drunk. You thought twice when somebody threatened to "get the IRA after you" for accidentally spilling a drink on their shoes. You may even have cheered in the pub when soldiers died. In short, your mentality was shaped and somewhat shamed by your proximity to the Border.

If some day the ragwort is cleared and the earthscar heals, and the bad times and the bad men are gone for

Unapproved Road

I

When we came to the customs post at Aughnacloy, as at
    Cullaville or Pettigoe,
I was holding my breath
as if I might yet again be about to go

underwater . . . the fortieth
anniversary of 1916 had somehow fizzled out, the New
    Year's Eve attack
on Brookeborough ending in the deaths

of O'Hanlon and South, while Dev was likely to bring back
internment without trial . . . As we drew
level with the levelled shack

I was met by another black-coated, long fellow, though he
    wore a sky-blue
winding-cloth or scarf
wrapped round his mouth and nose, leaving only a slit for
    him to peer through.

II

"In the late fifties I was looking for a place," he nestled his
    coffee-cup on its zarf
and turned to me, thirty years later, in Rotterdam . . .
"An ancestral place . . . A place my ancestors knew as
    Scairbh

good to be romanticised forever in song, I'll gladly sing "Four Roads to Glenamaddy" in a bath of Big Tom's sweat.

Sir George Quigley

After a career in the public service, Sir George Quigley joined the Board of Ulster Bank, of which he has been Chairman since 1989. He became Chairman of Shortt Bros. Ltd., part of the Bombardier Group, in May 1999. He is Chairman of the £11 billion NatWest Pension Fund. Sir George has recently been appointed President of the Economic and Social Research Institute, Dublin, and of the International Trade Institute of Ireland. He is a member of the Editorial Board of the Irish Banking Review *and delivered the Royal Dublin Society's Gold Medal Lecture in 1993. In 1997, he received the Compaq Lifetime Achievement Award for promoting cross-border economic co-operation. He is an Honorary Fellow of the Irish Management Institute and a Fellow of the Institute of Bankers.*

My first practical experience of North/South co-operation was in the 1960s, when I headed up the Government's Industrial Training Programme. We exchanged ideas, shared our solutions to problems, and participated in each other's arrangements for recruiting staff and providing them with experience. We were not in any way self-conscious about this. It was to mutual benefit. It seemed the most natural thing in the world.

My interest in the possibilities for North/South economic and business interaction was rekindled in the early
1990s when, as Chairman of Ulster Bank, I was invited to
contribute to a Conference organised by the Irish Association and, a little later, to speak on the theme of "the island
economy" at the Annual Conference of the Confederation
of Irish Industry (predecessor to Irish Business Employers
Confederation).

There was some suspicion at the time that a concept
such as this reflected a political agenda, whereas today
there is fairly widespread recognition that, on this island
as elsewhere, trade and investment flows follow their own
logic and ignore political boundaries. It has been reported
that one of the worst-kept secrets in Cyprus is that Greek
and Turkish farmers meet regularly at deserted parts of
the Green Line to trade goats and other animals.

There is no doubt, however, that even where borders
are not politically contentious and when there are no obvious impediments to trade, they constitute mental barriers that are only surmounted by conscious effort over
time. It has been calculated, for example, that six times
more trade takes place within countries in the European
Union than takes place between them. The Single Market
and EMU and the consequent reconfiguration of the
European economy are dismantling the barriers. Countries and regions all over Europe are eager to connect and
network, without losing their pride in their separate identities. It would be remarkable if similar tendencies had not
been displayed on this island.

And they have. The economic circuitry is steadily developing. Thanks to the effort of bodies like Co-operation
Ireland, employer and trade union organisations and

many other agencies, trade between the two parts of the island has been steadily growing and the Republic now takes a greater share of Northern Ireland's exports (nearly one-quarter) than any other country. The fact that the Republic is within the Eurozone and that the UK is outside has raised the stakes for the North's exporters but, even so, trade within the island is likely to have doubled by the tenth anniversary of the Single Market.

The more buoyant both economies are, the greater the prospects for each to benefit from the success of the other. For example, in a recent year, one-third of all US electronics investment in Europe, 45 per cent of software and 75 per cent of medical devices, was won by the Republic. To have such a chunk of the global economy within easy reach offers substantial opportunities to suppliers of intermediate goods and services in Northern Ireland.

I doubt, however, whether either part of the island has begun to capitalise on the strategic value of that proximity. As Northern Ireland liquidates the crippling liability of violence and political uncertainty, one could see overseas companies (particularly those already familiar with the island as an excellent host environment) widening the angle of their lens and regarding a location anywhere on the island, rather than elsewhere, as the best means of enhancing economies of scale. Friends in the South have suggested to me that this could be of considerable mutual benefit to North and South as the labour market in the South tightens. It would be a pity if either part of the island turned away investment that any part of the island could accommodate.

As an admirable recent study by the ESRI said, the co-operation project offering the best possible return probably lies in the field of energy. Both North and South are, on their own, too small to generate adequate competition or enable economies of scale to be reaped. Both would benefit from being part of an island energy market. Such was the conclusion of the Energy Working Group that I chaired as part of the recent 2010 Strategy project in Northern Ireland. It would *inter alia* entail co-ordinated planning of investment in transmission systems; agreement on terms of trade of energy for sale; and compatibility between the two systems of regulation.

Both parts of the island are at a critically formative phase in the development of energy policy and there is no time to be lost if the risk of their developing along ill-matched trajectories is to be avoided.

The same ESRI study to which I referred above stated a strong case for integrating the energy system of the Donegal area into the Northern Ireland system as part of an integrated programme for the development of the northwest of the island. That, of course, would also transform the economic prospects for the extension of the gas network within Northern Ireland.

We are steadily and pragmatically enlarging our understanding of the potential to capture island-wide synergies. The strides made in recent years in joint marketing of the island as a tourist destination is another example of co-operation which, in a normal environment, holds great promise.

Co-operation between areas on either side of the Border is vitally important as a fillip to economic growth. But it should not obscure the prizes to be won — and not least by the Border areas themselves — from an economic vision which encompasses the whole island. Far from being at the peripheries of their respective economies, they then form the geographic heart of what can be a vibrant island economy.

Janet Quilley

Janet Quilley is a member of the Religious Society of Friends. She worked for the Quakers in Belfast for six and a half years. She and her husband have recently re-turned to England to be closer to their family, but they maintain their keen interest in Irish affairs on both sides of the Border.

Reference to the Border reminds me of a back route from Dublin to Belfast we once travelled, thinking the road was open. Only when we reached the dead end did we realise why there was a proliferation of rabbits all over the road, and not a vehicle in sight for the last mile. The deeper significance of being so cut off with no cross-border traffic was an absence of casual contact between the communities, problems of access for farmers and general economic stagnation — quite apart from the general sense of unease, of suspicion rather than a welcome for strangers.

Asking a blow-in like me, with a mere six and half years' experience, to think about the meaning of the Border, might seem rather irrelevant. A land border has not been a political issue in Britain for centuries, although perhaps Hadrian's Wall and Offa's Dyke touch more raw nerves for the Scots and the Welsh than for the English.

Paddy Logue has commented that "the firmer the Border is, the more permeable it is". Borders become barriers when seen negatively as something to be challenged. They are the means of and reasons for obstruction, both physical and psychological. Barriers are forged by suspicion and insecurity; watchtowers and armed security forces are the hallmarks, whether on the Belfast–Dublin road or at Checkpoint Charlie in 1960s Berlin.

But the Border is more than a mere dividing line between two states. The symbolism of the Berlin Wall is repeated in the peace walls at interface areas in Belfast. It illustrates the real division between communities; it echoes the concern with national territory, expressing the suspicion and insecurity inherent in a relationship based on fear and threat. There is also a familiar replication of the economic stagnation and deprivation of the Border regions in the blighted areas around the peace lines, where houses are constantly attacked and vandalised and where people are driven out or choose in despair to move away. Regeneration is urgently needed but no one seems able to reverse the downward spiral.

There is a real sense in which the Border in all its manifestations needs to be firm so that it can be permeable. When people believe there is no hidden agenda, they can afford to make contacts across the Border, which they recognise as beneficial to themselves. Cross-border contact will take place on a pragmatic basis, developing in its own time rather than being forced. Nevertheless, it might well be open-ended and go further than people at present can envisage. Borders in the mind must be addressed first.

There must always be encouragement for other activities helping to forge links between North and South, which don't have a particularly cross-border connotation, but which in themselves lead to greater understanding, reducing suspicion and insecurity. We once encountered an endless stream of walkers in the Mournes, just as we thought we had got away from humankind. We discovered they were a mixed North-South group whose only agenda was an interest in hillwalking — there was a refreshing lack of high-sounding ideas about cross-border initiatives! Our Quaker meetings North and South are currently promoting opportunities for inter-visitation between individuals and families in order to share experience and nurture personal friendships. All the churches have structures that are ready-made for encouraging such contacts informally and without pressure.

Efforts to encourage positive relationships within Northern Ireland — across the urban interface areas and between different rural communities — will influence people's attitudes to the North/South Border. Community workers talk of single identity work, which is another way of talking about promoting security and self-confidence. A self-confident community of whatever persuasion in the North will more easily recognise the benefits of communication and co-operation, both with neighbouring communities and across the Border. Community development on each side of the Border and cross-border initiatives are equally essential, depending on each other for success.

Last summer I stood on top of Slemish in County Antrim. It had been on our list of Things-To-Be-Done before leaving Northern Ireland. Alas, that time had now come . . . The view from Slemish was memorable — a patchwork of fields firmly bounded by hedgerows fading into the distant mist. So many fields in England nowadays have lost their boundaries to the economics of large-scale commercial farming. The patchwork quilt is an appropriate image for Ireland, celebrating diversity — the more colour and vibrancy the better — whilst defining and maintaining the boundaries between the jigsaw pieces. Then there is a unifying lining, which acknowledges the interdependence of the individual pieces and how much they have in common. This is the European experience too, built up gradually and not without difficulty over the past 30 years; it makes sense in Ireland, North and South, as it does also in England, Scotland and Wales, within the wider European context.

Ruairi Quinn

Ruairi Quinn, TD, a Dubliner, trained as an architect/town planner in University College Dublin. He was elected as a Labour TD for Dublin South East in 1997. He has been a member of Dublin City Council and has held five different ministerial positions, the most recent being Labour's first Minister for Finance (1994–97). He was elected Leader of the Labour Party in 1997.

When I was a young child growing up in Dublin, my father's two sisters and their father lived across the Border in Warrenpoint. The Quinn family had migrated from rural County Down to Bootle, outside Liverpool, where my father was born, and then back to Newry in 1910. My mother grew up in what also became a Border town — Dundalk. My parents' marriage in 1936 was a truly cross-border affair!

In the early 1950s, rationing was still part of daily life in Warrenpoint when I came to stay with my grandfather and my aunts. Mars bars and spangles were the determining differences of life on the other side of the line, which we were told ran across the road at the Killeen Border station. Despite our best efforts, we could never see that line and yet we already knew when it was crossed.

In the summer, Sundays would see lifeboats from ships, converted into passenger ferries, move across Carlingford Lough from Warrenpoint to Omeath. Borders create differences in both supply and price. The boatmen, who would take on volunteer crew, easily met the demand for Free State butter or British produce.

Regional accents and foreign uniforms emphasised the different sides of the Border. The Orange hall, behind our house in Queen's Street, was to me a source of music, not bigotry. My grandfather was once horrified to see his grandsons gaily follow an Orange band down the street as it rehearsed for the Twelfth. It was useless to explain to him that we did not possess the magic of a marching band back in Sandymount.

My coming of age coincided with the most recent chapter of the Troubles. The Border became a menacing political security edifice of watchtowers, check posts and battle-hardened British soldiers. Their enquiries about our destination and purpose of our visit were usually courteous but always resented. The UDR asked similar questions, but in a familiar accent which was all the more threatening for that. Somehow it seemed totally wrong to be asked why you were coming home.

The graveyard, out the Warrenpoint Road, is the final resting place for many of the Quinn family, including my own brother who died at 18 months in 1939. My remaining aunt was now a patient in Daisyhill hospital and Newry a town changed beyond recognition.

My visits North, now, were political and sometimes on official Government business. The casual comfort of my uncle's car on its regular visit to his sisters in Warrenpoint was replaced with the discreet but cool protection of the RUC escort car.

How strange to be guarded on a visit to your father's place, I once thought as we sped up through Banbridge on the road to Belfast. Road signs and place names were constant reminders of being in the same place but across the Border. The landscape has no defining edge or dramatic change, yet the place certainly has. Tricolours and Union Jacks, along with painted kerbstones, defining internal territories, silently but loudly.

Then I wonder, remembering my father's explanations and exhortations, was the Border there before they put the station on the road at Killeen?

There are many borders across this small island. Some strong and natural, like the river Shannon at Limerick or Athlone, for example. Others divide cities like the north side and the south side between "them and us".

It is easier to cross over a border that is easily recognised and well defined, provided that both sides are open to visitors. In Ireland, I think we have been obsessed with one Border which, for all its faults, has never really been closed.

There are other borders which remain blocked, or at best, partially open across the rest of Ireland. These are the borders that remain invisible to the keepers yet monumental to those enclosed. They are not physical borders, easily defined or dangerous to touch, like the barbed wire around the defensive watchtowers. But their tracks criss-cross this land and all the people who today live upon it.

When borders become recognised for what they really are — divisions that stand in the way of liberty — then the task of reconciliation and empowerment can at last begin.

Solving the problem of the Border is a task that concerns not just the North and the South, but the East and the West as well.

Social prejudice, racial fears, economic poverty and social exclusion, such as adult illiteracy or homelessness, are reinforced by the borders which have been erected across the back of the Celtic Tiger.

Derek Reaney

Derek Reaney was born and has lived all his life at the foot of the Sperrin Mountains near the village of Plumbridge, County Tyrone. He is a part-time hill farmer and a full-time development officer for Derry and Raphoe Action, a cross-border organisation which aims to encourage Protestant communities to play an active role in community development processes in the rural areas of Counties Tyrone, Londonderry and Donegal, and to develop cross-border networks.

As a child looking at a map of Ireland, the Border was a deep red line dividing Northern Ireland from the Republic of Ireland. My grandfather originally came from County Wicklow. He served in the Royal Irish Constabulary and when partition came he was stationed in Londonderry, where he lived for the rest of his life, except for four and a half years spent as a prisoner of war in a camp in Poland. He had a great Southern accent, something he kept all through his life, and I can always remember him saying, "I wouldn't give a match to the Free State". He lived until he was 85 and never again crossed the Border. He very rarely talked about his family or his time spent in County Wicklow, but he did tell us about his brothers and how they were killed by republicans in the 1920s Troubles.

This is a family story almost 80 years old, and in the years that lie ahead, similar stories will be told of what has happened during the last 30 years of terror. Although I was brought up and still live just nine miles from the Border, at the foot of the Sperrins in County Tyrone, my family never crossed the Border for the simple reason of security. My father spent 30 years in uniform — 20 years in the "B" Specials and ten years in the UDR. It was simply too dangerous for him, and many others like him, to cross the Border.

As a child growing up during the 1970s, the Border, and what existed on the other side were dark and evil. I saw the Border as somewhere for terrorists to run behind. Where they could be safe beyond the reach of the security forces. A place they could plan, train and launch their murderous campaign.

The terror campaign, which was aimed at the removal of the Border and the unification of Ireland, only helped to widen the border between people and secure the Border's physical presence.

During the mid-1980s, we crossed the Border two or three times a year. The Republic seemed different — different road signs, different attitudes and different ethos. Over the last few years, the physical appearance of the Border has changed. In most cases it is simply like crossing from County Tyrone into County Fermanagh. The apparatus of security has disappeared, but the Border lives on and will remain to live on for generations to come.

Today, probably the most noticeable difference is the currency, and with the advent of the euro, this difference has continued to grow.

While things change, the reason for the Border remains unchanged — fear coupled with lack of respect and understanding. The Border is a symbol for the problems in this island. Two different communities, two different peoples and two different cultures.

The Border is blamed for many things: poverty, economic depression, dividing people and families and even

communities and villages. For those who are from a unionist position, the Border is a line in the sand, a full stop
behind which we can be free. Perhaps a nationalist would
rather use the words "dominate and control", but surely
the Roman Catholic Church controlled and dominated the
Irish Republic? Perhaps things have changed in recent
years, or have they?

In August 1998, I returned for a visit to Newtown-
mountkennedy, County Wicklow, with my wife and children. We visited the church and graveyard and saw the
headstone of my great-grandmother and my two great-
uncles. We had planned to stay two weeks on the south-
east coast, but at the end of the first week, on Saturday, 15
August, we left, wanting to get home after hearing the
news of the Omagh bomb. As we crossed the Border at
Aughnacloy at about 2.00 a.m. in the morning, still an
hour and a half away from home, my wife said to me,
"Thank God we are home."

The 29 people who lost their lives in Omagh are added
to the long list of those who have been murdered in the
name of Irish unity. It is quite ironic that those who wish
the Border removed have done so much to maintain it —
both physically and, perhaps more importantly, mentally.

The Border will remain for many years to come. It may
from time to time become a little blurred at the edges, and
if and when it disappears, it will remain in the hearts of
men and women.

Today that red line on the map is not just ink, it is
blood, sacrificed in the name of peace and freedom and it
will simply not disappear as easily as some would wish.

Mary Reid

Mary Reid is a community worker, writer, teacher and researcher. She is fascinated by borders and boundaries — the imaginative legacy of a childhood spent between the shores of Lough Derg and Lough Erne. She believes with our ancestors, the ancient Celts, that we live in a universe constructed of parallel worlds. She lives in hope that Einstein, too, was right and that we will come to discover that parallel worlds really do meet in infinity.

In memory of Plunkett Reid, 18 October 1999
I grew up in a Border village. This turns out to be a blessing, but mostly I have lived it as a curse. I do not belong. In the South, I am considered a Northerner, argumentative, troublesome. In the North, I am seen as a Southerner, inclined to the soft option, never completely trusted by anyone in the jungle of coded cries. I have grown up shorn of that shell (hell?) that is fundamental to the Irish psyche — a sense of community. In consequence, I have spent my life seeking the elusive key to belonging. I have searched the streets of ghettos, I have searched in mountain streams. With Patrick Kavanagh, another outsider, I confess to having "tested and tasted too much . . . Struggle, Striving . . .". It has all the same salty aftertaste now, the taste of tears. I have come to prefer the bland, precious, life-giving tastelessness of water.

A while ago, I sat in a top Dublin restaurant "selling" Ireland to travel writers. The mess on my plate cost one hundred pounds. Ultimately, PAYE workers somewhere will pay for it. I wondered why the celebrity chef, wearing his celebrated scowling face, did not adorn the concoction with an edible price tag? In the den of the Celtic Tiger, conspicuous consumption is the new credo. This new wealth must be seen to sheen on our bodies, adorn our nakedness, slither through our intestines. Meanwhile, around the corner, in Harcourt Street, in Georgian mansions turned into slum tenements, the whey-faced pallor of the children of the poor haunt the city, as they always have done. As the New Ireland glimmered and shone about me, teenagers ingested one hundred pound doses of white powdered death. They will never grow up to be PAYE workers. I do not want to belong here.

Some weeks later, I stepped off a plane in Belfast City Airport. I turned to the father of a family I met while on holiday. He was a quiet, gentle man, whose own happiness was the pleasure his family took in the sun and the sea. I turned to that man on the top step of that plane and saw a light go out in his eyes. The dank grey Belfast air, groaning under the drumbeat of lost causes and a forgotten empire, swirled down to claim us. Within a week, a young man nicknamed "Chucky" would be brought to waste ground, blindfolded, shot in the head, and laid in his grave. *Tiocfaidh, Tiocfaidh, Tiocfaidh.* . . . I do not want to belong here.

I read the local paper, having long ago abandoned any interest in real news. My brain goes numb at the Tweedledum Tweedledee patter on offer. Again, with Kavanagh, I am consoled by the abiding epic in the merely local. Three shining faces smile out at me. I smile back at them. They attended the same school as I did in the Border village. They too stared up at that fading, mysterious, magical map of the world that still hangs on the classroom wall and wondered, as I did, if one day they would visit that faraway world. They grew up, crossed the Border and now, with deserved happiness and pride, announce that they possess doctorates and degrees in specialities I cannot even pronounce. They are the future. With their knowledge, skill and application, the mirage on the classroom wall sits in the palm of their hands.

They will never know the tyranny of the local. They need never fear nor seek favour from the local power broker, a politician with a brain the size of a sheep's, but the guile and cunning of a viper (if decent cold-blooded vipers everywhere will excuse me the comparison). I think of their parents who have worked so much for this moment, who, like all those parents, the forgotten people in the underbelly of the Celtic Tiger, struggle and persevere in order to give their children the freedom to belong here or elsewhere, on equal terms.

Tiocfaidh, Tiocfaidh, Tiocfaidh . . . there is only one place we are all travelling towards and that is to the future . . . but like pagan sun worshippers we know not to stare too directly at our golden destination. After all, there we must die. As a child, my favourite place in that Border village was a hidden spot by the river in the no-man's-land that ran between the North and South. There I would sit behind the veil of a waterfall and watch the matchstick world unfolding in the distance. That remains my favourite place. When the Border reopened after a quarter of a century, I returned and discovered a riot of flowers, butterflies and water-living things. Nature had thrived in our absence. Only Travellers shared that place; it was where they chose to camp. There, I am told, I was often found eating by the campfire at bedtime. There I belong, in the "no-place" we call Utopia.

So I will tell you this about borders. The greatest border we have to cross is the border we come to when we look at ourselves. Sit on a park bench, or in your garden, or at the breakfast table, look inside yourself. If you find it is good, then you are already making the crossing. I believe unlikely things. I am coming to believe that it is possible to become good by virtue of a process of elimination. Try Belief, try Love, try Loss. Then try just Living. If my theory holds water, than we have much to look forward to. In any event, we will all come to that inevitable destination in the future, where needs must, we will all belong.

Rev. Dr Andrew Rodgers

Dr Andrew Rodgers was born in 1930 at the Manse in Lisburn, where his father was the Minister. He was educated at Magee College, Derry, and Trinity College, Dublin, where he gained an MA. He has ministered in Belfast, Glaslough, Clones, Ballyhobridge, Stonebridge and Newbliss, Dungannon. He was Moderator of the General Assembly of the Presbyterian Church in Ireland, 1993–1994. He has three children and four grandchildren.

What is the Border? That which divides the North from the South, geographically, culturally, and economically. I write simply as a clergyman glad that my Church, "The Presbyterian Church in Ireland", knows no boundaries or borders.

I spent the first seven and a half years of my ministerial service in Clones, close to the Monaghan/Fermanagh

Border. The remaining 30-plus years were spent in Dungannon, and in 1993–94, as Moderator of the Presbyterian Church in Ireland, I sought to minister to all our members both north and south of the Border.

My years in Clones left me in no doubt regarding the answer to the question "What is the Border?" It was, to me and many of my parishioners, a daily *burden* of considerable proportions. My four small congregations were scattered across the Border, with roads blocked because of the IRA campaign of the late 1950s and early 1960s. Journeys to families across the Border required major detours (16 miles instead of 5 to go to Rosslea).

Pressed into service, though ill equipped, I also taught in Clones High School, a small Protestant grammar school with only around 60 pupils serving the rural community from both sides of the Border. This meant I had to prepare pupils for Intermediate and Leaving Certificate or Junior and Senior Certificate. Two examinations, instead of four, would have been so much more manageable. The Border was a *burden*. Yet, from that small school many were equipped for life, some entering the various professions, including a recent Presbyterian Moderator and a County Monaghan TD.

Yes! The Border was a burden. As I had never been taught Irish, the Government would not fund me as a teacher, and so I was paid only what the school governors could afford — £3 per week — probably much more than I was worth! Yet I knew just a few miles north, it would have been £25 per week!

But while the Border could be burdensome, it was not always so. In due course, I received income tax forms, which, being printed in Irish, were even more incomprehensible than those I formerly received in the North. For a while, I ignored or neglected them until I received a form which demanded my attention and response. Instead of attempting to fill it in, I wrote a letter stating my salary as a minister, £420, and as a teacher £150. I included my travel expenses and details of my dependants — wife and daughter — finishing with the simple question, "What do I owe you?" By return, I received a printed document on which was written at the bottom "Nothing, God help you!" I couldn't imagine a similar response from Belfast. The Border had its *blessings*.

Recently, my wife and I traveled from Portadown to Cork on two excellent express trains, enjoying the comfort, ease and pleasure of the five-hour journey, and at no cost to us as pensioners — thanks to the Border.

My daughter was trained as a Doctor in University College Dublin and was known by her many friends as the unique one of the hundred Protestants out of the ten thousand students at the University, in that her father was a "Protestant priest". No Border of *bigotry* there! Many of her student colleagues from the South received no grant and had to work in part-time and holiday jobs to fund themselves through college, while Alison had a grant which covered her bills. The Border was a *boon* to her and a *burden* to them.

Later, my son was involved in some serious cross-border activity and became engaged to an O'Donnell lassie from Dublin, causing concern in some Northern quarters, until the wedding invitations arrived to prove that O'Donnells can be Episcopalians. Is it the Border that exposes our *bigotry* or our bigotry that exposes the Border?

As moderator of our Church in 1993–94, I visited all the security bases along the length of the Border as well as many of the Presbyterian farming communities in that area. Those visits left me with the indelible impression of terrible tension, strain, danger, death, and a sense of siege experienced by people for whom the Border was simply "Bandit Country!"

I am also very aware that the Border is rapidly changing in many areas of life. Passing through Dublin Airport, I visited a gents' toilet and found myself staring in utter disbelief at what must surely be one of the most tangible signs of that change — a contraceptive vending machine. What next!?

As a Northerner and as a Presbyterian, I wish to put on record that I have always found warmth, respect, courtesy and friendship extended to me wherever I went along the Border, North or South.

The recent emergence of the "Celtic Tiger", aided by EU grants and evidenced by vast improvements in roads, agriculture, industry — indeed, in the whole standard of living — now makes the Border, which used to divide the "prosperous North" from the "poor South" virtually *irrelevant* economically.

So what is the Border? Is it a burden; a blessing; bigotry; bandit country; an irrelevance?

It is my hope and prayer that, in the years to come, the answer to that question will be "a bridge". A bridge to link the two parts of Ireland, though very different in history, culture and religion; a bridge to link them in economic, industrial and social co-operation for mutual benefit, friendship and enrichment.

Nick Ross

Nick Ross is a broadcaster, chiefly with the BBC, best known as the presenter of Crimewatch UK. *He special-ised in Irish affairs in the 1970s and retains a strong link with Northern Ireland. His documentary* We Shall Over-come *won the 1999 best documentary prize at the Gaelic Film Festival. He was a British Radio Broadcaster of the Year in 1997 for his long-running current affairs phone-in* Call Nick Ross.

The Irish question had been solved in 1921. The Catholics would have the South, Protestants the North, Britain free at last. So for me, a south London boy arriving in Belfast as a student in 1965, the Irish Border, the real one, was not the shaded line on maps round Ballyshannon and Dundalk. It ran down the Irish Sea.

I felt I was abroad. True, the road signs were familiar in the North, but there was a brittle atmosphere, a meanness of spirit that would scarcely have been recognised in Eng-land since Victorian times. For God's sake, municipal swings were chained up on the Sabbath. In the South, there was literally a veneer of green (what struck me most on my first trip to Dublin was that somewhere south of Newry, the pillar boxes and phone kiosks were no longer painted red); but there too, Christianity seemed to be a stifling rather than emancipating influence.

In the swinging sixties, we Brits in Ireland must have seemed disconcertingly liberal and non-conformist. In the North, my friends were more likely to be Catholic; in the South, Protestants.

For Irish people too, the real Border was the sea. For those who travelled at all, going North or South was nothing very special, but travelling to England seemed a real journey. Britain was another country.

So it was that when the Troubles flared in 1968 and 1969, the British were bewildered. Thirty years ago, neither Whitehall nor Fleet Street knew anything much about Ireland, and had little concept of political partition or the religious divide. Most people, if they had a view at all, thought the Irish hard-drinking but good-natured. There were jokes about the Irish, just as there were about the Germans or Jews, but it was light-hearted – the joshing about rural naivety that you hear just as readily in pubs in Dublin. As with all jokes based on stereotype, good nature can quickly turn to malice, yet even at the worst of the bombing campaign in the 1970s and 1980s, Britons were not so much hostile to Ireland as generally perplexed.

The Irish, North and South, Catholic and Protestant, find things simpler because they share a profound sense of colonial history.

Indeed, many Irish men and women have a dependency on Britain still, like the teenager who has left home but still blames mum and dad for everything, and still looks to them to sort things out. Not only unionists cling to the skirts of Great Britain; so too do many nationalists and almost all republicans. Most curious, most ironic, most rooted in a preposterous blindness to what has changed, has been Sinn Féin. The Provisional IRA emerged as a result of Britain's abject failure to govern Northern Ireland properly – indeed, its failure to govern it at all. Yet their demands have always been absurd. They wanted British troops out at a time when only the presence of British servicemen prevented widespread ethnic cleansing. They bombed, shot and intimidated their Protestant neighbours and expected the British to "persuade" them that the IRA were really their good friends. They still talk of Britain as a colonial power in Ireland, yet it is a strange imperialism that, instead of living off its colony, pours in money and resources. The Provos cling to a colonial analysis because without it they would have no cause; they would have to concede that their quarrel is with fellow Irish men and women.

Indeed, had Britain acted in a more colonial way in the 1950s and 1960s, reforming Stormont or even governing from London, the latest Troubles might never have begun. How ironic that the Catholics were urging British intervention and the British were reluctant to get involved. When eventually the troops went in, belatedly and clumsily, Ireland's quarrels seemed alien. Unionist jingoism seemed deeply un-British; the riots and bombing revived centuries-old images of the Irish as primitives. So Irish stereotypes of the British became self-fulfilling: the soldiers began to act like an occupying force; as British soldiers got killed, the London media began baying like colonial bigots of old; and English courts began meting out second-rate justice to the savages.

Die-hard old-fashioned unionists find it hard to accept, but the latest Troubles developed over civil rights, not partition. Die-hard old-fashioned republicans find it hard to accept, but the argument about the reunification of Ireland has not advanced one jot for all their endeavours, and North/South collaboration has been set back by their violence. The frontier may raise foolish patriotic passions, but it is not partition that divides the people of Ireland. It is prejudice.

Wealth will be a healer. People who succeed have less need of scapegoats than people who are poor. In parts of the North, but especially in the South of Ireland, narrow attitudes nurtured by poverty have given way to a more relaxed self-confidence. Perhaps it is the greatest reason for hope that after centuries in Britain's shadow, Ireland can be so at ease, so self-assured. It no longer needs to bolster its esteem by demonising someone else. One day, I hope not far away, Britons will look across the Irish Sea to see neighbours who are more prosperous than they are and more secure about their identity and future. Then, when the Irish no longer feel inferior, and the British are no longer supercilious, and only then, will Ireland's most enduring border disappear: across the Irish Sea will be people who regard themselves as equals.

Rev. Kenneth Wilson

Ken Wilson was born in 1939 in Belfast. He trained for the Methodist Ministry at Edgehill College, Belfast, followed by missionary work in the West Indies. Returning to Ireland, he has served in Cullybackey, Glenburn (Belfast), Lisburn and Bray. Ken has two children by his first wife, Bertha, who died in 1993. He was married to Ruth in 1997. In June 1999, he was installed as President of the Methodist Church in Ireland and will hold office for one year.

The fact that I have never really thought much about this subject before may come as a surprise to those who seem to define who they are in terms of the Border. What I shall say in this article is a personal view, and will not reflect the views of everyone in my Church. I write as a Christian, and this implies that, far and away above any other allegiance, my primary allegiance is to Jesus Christ. Because of the strange way in which our culture and our faith have become intertwined, I feel I must point out that my views on the Border are not fundamental to my standing as a Christian. While nationalists wish to see the end of the Border, unionists wish to see it strengthened. I have close friends in both camps whose commitment to the Lordship of Jesus is beyond question.

My thinking has been shaped by several things:

1. My childhood was spent in Dungannon and Armagh and Belfast, and I have no memory of my family debating much about the Border. I suppose I was never a dyed-in-the-wool Ulsterman. On my father's side, my family had come from Scotland at the turn of the

century to tend sheep on the Mourne Mountains. And on my mother's side, I think, my family had lived and worked for a while on the railway south of the Border. Perhaps this would explain why I was never under any pressure as I grew up to have any strong feelings towards the Border. It was there, and you had to have you car-pass stamped when you went to the other side. But that was about it!

2. My attitude was shaped by embracing the evangelical Christian faith. I suppose that when many Protestant teenagers in Ulster were being drawn into groups like the Orange Order, I was captivated by the two great loves of my life — sport and a desire to follow Jesus. Roger Bannister has been the first to break the "four-minute mile", and I wanted to follow him. But Jesus became an even greater Hero. In my youthful enthusiasm, I wanted to save the world for Jesus Christ. I saw that all people were equally loved by God, and I felt under an obligation to pass on to others the wonder of a personal relationship with Jesus Christ. The only "border" worth discussing was that which separated men and women from God! Before entering Edgehill Theological College in Belfast, I was posted to the Dublin Central Mission in George's Street for a year. I fell in love with Dublin. It was a strange new world for someone who had gone to school in Portadown. The policeman (guard!) on points duty at O'Connell Bridge; the swarms of bicycles with their engines to drive the front wheels; the smells of the breweries and the Liffey; and the warm-hearted Methodist people — it took my breath away. Despite what some Northerners had told me, I had as much freedom to preach and

evangelise as in the North. Ever since, my concern has been more about the Kingdom of God rather than the United Kingdom. Earthly kingdoms will pass; His will last forever.

3.   After training in Belfast, I spent 12 years in the West Indies, where I had to contend with "borders" such as colour, education, class, money. It was during this time that the "Troubles" began. It was a salutary thing to look at my homeland from the other side of the world and realise that it is not the centre of the universe. Ireland is a tiny speck on the world map. I was called upon to explain my West Indian friends what was happening back home. I began to think: "What right have I to preach peace and love in a strange land when my countrymen cannot settle their differences in a civilised way?" I returned to Ireland about 20 years ago, and I have been confirmed in my belief that by far the more serious "border" is the one in our hearts. I feel that anything that hinders people from hearing the story of the reconciling love of God is to be questioned. It would not cost me a second thought if tomorrow the Border between North and South were to disappear, provided I had the same freedom that I have today to address the problem of the age-old "border" in our hearts.

I began saying that this is a personal view. I have a deep respect for those who see things differently. What saddens me is that there is a form of Christianity that may judge my standing as a Christian simply on what I think about the Border.